TWO QUIET LIVES

Dorothy Osborne
Thomas Gray

also by David Cecil

THE STRICKEN DEER
or the Life of Cowper

HARDY, THE NOVELIST
The Clark Lectures
delivered at Cambridge, 1942

EARLY VICTORIAN NOVELISTS
Essays in Revaluation of
Dickens, Thackeray, the Brontes
Trollope, George Eliot and
Mrs. Gaskell

THE YOUNG MELBOURNE
and the story of his marriage
with Caroline Lamb

DAVID CECIL

Two Quiet Lives

Barbara Jones

CONSTABLE

To
The Lady Desborough
"La Reine des Reines"

LONDON
PUBLISHED BY
Constable and Company Ltd.
10–12 ORANGE STREET, W.C.2

·

INDIA
Longmans, Green and Company Ltd.
BOMBAY CALCUTTA MADRAS

·

CANADA
Longmans, Green and Company Ltd.
TORONTO

First published . . . 1948

PRINTED IN GREAT BRITAIN BY THE CHISWICK PRESS
NEW SOUTHGATE, LONDON, N.11

PREFATORY NOTE

THESE studies are not a work of research. All the information in them is already in print. But the two characters, who are their subject, seem to me curious and complex enough to deserve a closer analysis and a more extended interpretation than they have up to now received. Further, they illustrate with unusual clearness a peculiar and interesting variety of the human temperament. For, widely as their characters differed in many important respects, temperamentally they were akin. Both were shy, anxious, pensive personalities, with a rich inner life and few but intense affections, who, inspired by an ineradicable distrust of the world, strove, with varying success, to retire from it to a life exclusively personal, private, contemplative. The character that such a life assumed for each of them was not quite the same; for it was modified by the fact that they lived in different ages and different societies. In fact, it is not possible to understand Gray or Dorothy without having first learnt to understand the worlds in which their lives were set. My book, then, aspires to be at once an account of two remarkable persons, a study of a certain phase of human nature and, finally, a picture of private life as lived in two contrasting periods.

My thanks are due to the Viscountess Mountbatten, to the Lord Walpole and to the Trustees of the National Portrait Gallery and of the Fitzwilliam Museum, Cambridge, for their great kindness in allowing me to reproduce portraits in their possession.

DAVID CECIL

vii

CONTENTS

ILLUSTRATIONS

Part One

DOROTHY OSBORNE

"When I am gone, dreame me some happinesse
Nor let thy looks our long hid love confesse."

JOHN DONNE

DOROTHY OSBORNE

I

ANTHEA, Lucasta, Castara, Sacharissa—the lady loves of the cavalier poets certainly have romantic names: and they look romantic too, gazing down at us in pearly satin and pensive grace from the canvases of Lely and Vandyck. But were they in reality romantic persons? Ah! that is hard to say: indeed it is hard to imagine them as human beings at all. The art that has made them celebrated has also concealed their humanity. After all, they cannot always have worn satin. Nor in fact were they known to their friends by these fanciful names. They were called Margaret or Mary, or Jane. But of Margaret and Mary and Jane, of these ladies in their everyday flesh and blood reality, we know little. We have no idea how they would have struck us, if we had found ourselves next to them at the dinner table. Always a curtain of splendid ceremony hangs between them and us; their voices are always drowned by a concert of elaborate lyrical music. Always—but for one exception: in the letters of Dorothy Osborne, the music is hushed, the curtain drawn aside. We hear Anthea's voice in ordinary conversation, we get a glimpse of Lucasta's real face.

It is only a glimpse. The correspondence covers no more than a few months of its author's life. Moreover, it is a narrow glimpse. Since Dorothy's letters are the only full record we have of her circle, she is the only figure in it that is steadily illuminated. Its other members remain shadowy and indistinct, save when they emerge for a moment into the clear candlelight of her vision. But her own personality is revealed

3

in intimate detail, and during the course of the supreme crisis of her life. So that the correspondence does not give us a feeling of incompleteness. By a freak of fortune this slender chance-kept bundle of letters has composed itself into a brief drama that has the unity and concentration and harmony of a conscious work of art.

Its setting is the world of aristocratic country life during the first years of the Commonwealth. In some ways English high life does not seem to have altered much since then. Here we are in a country house. The gentlemen, just in from hunting, are starting to argue about politics; the ladies, bent over their needlework, gossip about the shocking conduct of Lady Mary Sandys in appearing publicly with her lover Colonel Paunton at Winchester Races. On the other hand we notice with surprise that they take it as quite natural that the gentlemen of their acquaintance should have been fighting a duel, and that they have all, so they say, been drinking beer at breakfast. Their dresses are not very clean; when a visitor comes in they sink to the ground in a magnificent curtsy; while in the corner of the room, a girl is writing to her lover in words of accomplished poetical eloquence. All this is not very like the high life we know.

Indeed, this society presents such a bewildering blend of the familiar and the unexpected that it is hard at first to get one's bearings in it. Its conditions of living were primitive and home-made. People remained for years together buried in the country, subsisting on food grown on their own land, and dwelling in houses built by their own workmen. Countesses superintended jam-making and counted the holes in their husbands stockings; if the house was full of visitors, the hostess thought nothing of packing three ladies of title into one bed; the arrival of a new book was a rare event, only one uncertain post came and went in the week. People, most of them, were of a piece with the way they lived, normal, ingenuous, un-

4

inhibited, their interests revolving round the elemental facts of birth and death and marriage. Their feelings were ardent and unsophisticated, their speculations full of wonder and ignorance. Even sceptical Sir Thomas Browne believed in witches. Educated people would recommend each other to take powdered mummy by moonlight as the cure for an ailment. Nobody was afraid of uttering a platitude. "Youth is the time for love", they told one another, "death comes equally to all". Indeed, death did loom insistently before them. Medical science was as primitive as household management; and, though couples often had thirteen children, it was seldom that more than a few of them lived to grow up. Their parents lamented their loss with biblical extravagance, but took it very much as a matter of course. For their life was too close to the earth for them to be unrealistic about it. The cavalier gentry accepted the plain facts of existence without questioning. Money for instance, and all the solid security that money implied, mattered to them a great deal. They never married without it; they generally married to get it. And, though they felt the family bond very strongly, the closest relations would squabble for years about the terms of a dowry or an inheritance.

Yet they were not materialists. Their outlook was made spiritual by the sublime background of religious belief, against which they envisaged it. Man was an immortal soul; and his sojourn on this planet was but the brief prelude to an eternity of earthly bliss, or torment, to which he was destined according as to how far he had attained to true virtue. Their idea of virtue, too, was exalted and spacious, appreciative of every nicety of conscience, every impulse of magnanimity. Their hearts glowed for honour, for chivalry, for the excellent passion of friendship, the divine flame of love, the high mystery of virginity. With moral sensibility went sensibility of the imagination. They delighted in beauty. Did they not adorn themselves with velvet and lace and lovelocks perfumed with orange flower? Their walls were rich with carving and pictures; they wrote verses and sang them to the lute; they planted gardens to refresh the troubled spirit; their religion expressed itself in the jewelled and courtly mode of George Herbert. This idealism and this artistic sense combined to incarnate themselves in their way of living. Life they felt should have a noble and rhetorical form. Manners were ceremonious. The lover fell on his knees; the mourner draped his room with black cloth; boys and girls alike were taught to move with courtly dignity. Conduct too was regulated by a strict code of convention. Everybody had their place in the hierarchy of society and was expected to behave in a manner befitting it. Children must not marry without their parents' consent, women must obey their husbands; a duke was a duke, a commoner was a commoner, and must conduct themselves as such. Nor did people resent these rules as imposing a check on their lawful freedom. For they did not believe in convention—as later ages did—because they thought it helped life to function smoothly. Their faith was sacramental; convention was the outward and visible sign of their inward and spiritual sense of values. A man owed it to himself as much as to society to keep to it. Openly to flout convention, to imperil public reputation, was to him almost as heinous a crime as it is to the Japanese; it was an offence against his personal ideal of what he ought to be.

This mixture of primitive simplicity and formalized behaviour made their life lacking in variety. Surely it must have been monotonous to live in a world where so much was taken for granted, and where there were so few things to think about. On the other hand their existence was far more integrated than ours. They felt no awkward dissonance between the ideal and the real, the poetic and the prosaic. They did not distinguish between a man's public and his private personality. Accepting equally the earthly and the spiritual, their vision embraced all experience in one harmony. They wrote a lyric, and called on the name of God, and went to law about a will with the same unembarrassed wholeheartedness. Further, the fact that they were undisturbed by complex and heterogeneous issues enabled them to cultivate to the finest perfection those qualities they did value. Their poetry had a narrow range of theme, but it was the poetry of Lovelace and Vaughan; their music, confined within a few rigid forms, was yet the subtle polyphony of Orlando Gibbons. Naïve intellectually, they achieved an exquisite civilization of the heart. The naïveté enhanced the exquisiteness. It was their child-like lack of self-consciousness that allowed them to pray and converse and make love with so richly decorated a beauty. And they had the peculiar charm which comes from a refinement so natural as to be unaware of itself. How it speaks from the portraits of the age with their shy distinction, their silvery candour of glance! More profoundly aristocratic than their descendants of the eighteenth century, their good breeding seemed so fundamental as to be a quality of the soul. Yet there was always something homely and countrified about them. Through the mullioned casement open to the air, a whiff of cowslip breathes in to linger freshly amid the tapestry and the panelling.

This society reached its most delicate flowering in the early years of Charles I's reign. The blaze of the Elizabethan noonday had faded to a cooler gleam. Some of the old magnificent exuberance was gone; but its loss was balanced by an increased fastidiousness of sensibility. Instead of Marlowe there was Marvell; instead of the flamboyance of the Jacobean mansion, the classic grace of Inigo Jones; and among the more sensitive spirits of the time, we can discern, beneath their ceremoniousness of demeanour, hints of a new feeling for the pleasures of intimacy, of retirement, of introspection. Alas, it was not to be satisfied. The crash of violent political conflict broke in upon their world. The victory of the Parliamentary forces undermined that aristocratic supremacy which was necessary for the security of their existence. Sons and brothers fell in battle; fortunes were lost or confiscated; the country houses, in which their ideal of private life found its shrine, were sequestrated from their owners. Even if a man managed to shelter himself from the full shock of the storm, its rumour reverberated always in the distance, its shadow brooded darkly over the landscape. An uneasy sadness pervaded the spirit.

II

The Osborne family felt it. The war had found them in a position which, if not splendid, was solidly prosperous and dignified. Peter Osborne, head of an old-established Bedfordshire family had, like his father and grandfather before him, devoted his life to the public service; with such effect that at the age of fifty-eight he was a Knight, Governor of the Island of Guernsey, the husband of a Baronet's daughter, and the possessor of an income of £4,000 a year. Three of his children, it is true, had died; but since five survived, their loss did not, by the standards of the day, constitute much of a blot on his good fortune. Nor did the variety of his activities interfere with the amenity of his existence. Serving the State then was a much more easy-going affair than it is now; and, after doing his work in Guernsey and London, Sir Peter still had plenty of time left to spend at his family home of Chicksands, near Bedford.

But the moment the war broke out, his luck began to turn. A fine old cavalier gentleman, all sturdy loyalty and high-spirited honour, he did not hesitate which side to take. No more Chicksands for him, for the time being; he was off to Guernsey, prepared to hold it for his King till the last breath was out of his body. He very nearly had to. Guernsey rose in support of the Parliament; and the King's garrison was driven into the rocky citadel of Castle Cornet, where they remained in a state of siege for the rest of the war. The long lonely defence of this outpost of the Crown was a heroic exploit. It was also a thankless one. For Sir Peter, like so many supporters of the Stuart family, got worse than no help from his own side. Colonel Carteret, Governor of Jersey, intrigued incessantly against him; while Charles I's failure to send assistance of any kind, in spite of piteous demands for it, was made particularly irritating by his characteristic habit of writing frequently to say he was sending some at once. Sir Peter did his best to get supplies locally, only to have them confiscated on the way for his own use by Colonel Carteret. However Sir Peter's spirit was not quelled. He pawned his own clothes to get other provisions; and though the leader of the Parliamentary forces often proposed generous terms of surrender, he repudiated his offers in terms of resounding defiance. "God, I hope" he proclaimed, "whose great name I have sworn by, will never so much forsake me, but that I shall keep that resolution—by yourself misnamed obstinacy—to maintain unto my Sovereign that faith inviolate to the last."

Inspired by his fortitude, for four years in the wild sea-girt fortress, exposed alike to the onslaught of their enemies and the gales and breaking seas of the channel, the little garrison hung on, though they were forced to break up the doors for firewood and their bread ration was sometimes reduced to four biscuits a week. And then, after all, Colonel Carteret's intrigues succeeded. Sir Peter got word giving him gracefully to understand that the King would be glad if he resigned. "I pray you" he replied with courteous bitterness "to grant my direct going to St. Malo, where I may for a while quietly recollect myself and recover some patience for what I suffer and foresee I am still like to do."

The news from home was not such as to revive his spirits. His third surviving son had been killed early in the war; he had spent a large part of his fortune in the defence of Castle Cornet; his house was taken over by the Parliament and his family turned homeless into the world. Poor Lady Osborne had toiled with her children over to St. Malo, the nearest she could get to Guernsey, where she had thrown herself manfully into the task of selling the family plate to get supplies for Sir Peter, and writing letters to influential persons in England complaining about Colonel Carteret. Her health, however, had given way under the strain, and after a year or two she had returned to her own country, where she eked out a dreary life trailing about from relation to relation and often compelled to seek refuge in the uncomfortable atmosphere of a Roundhead brother's house in Chelsea. By the time Sir Peter was ejected from Guernsey, it was not safe for him to go back to an England now mainly under Parliamentary control. He remained at St. Malo for three years in extreme poverty, gloomily watching from across the Channel the final defeat of his party. The execution of Charles I brought his situation to a crisis; he learnt that if he did not make terms with his enemies, Chicksands would be confiscated for ever. Very reluctantly he sat down and wrote a dignified letter to Charles II, explaining that, in spite of the fact that his loyalty was still unshaken, he saw no way but to submit. He paid a large portion of the remains of his fortune in return for the right to live retired in his country home, and sailed for England. As a crowning misfortune, his wife died within a year of his returning. By 1652, however, all this was a thing of the past. The clash of battle had died away, and the life of the Osborne family was settled into a muted melancholy. Sir Peter was still alive; but he was now a very old man, his health and spirits alike broken by all he had gone through, his friends exiled and impoverished, and himself reduced to an income of £400 a year,

lingering out his last days down at Chicksands in an England, over which Cromwell and his Major Generals seemed to have established a permanent dictatorship. Now and again a relation came to visit him; but most of the time he lived alone there with his youngest child, the twenty-two year old Dorothy.

Chicksands was a fitting setting for such an existence. The grey rambling low-storied old house, with its mediaeval stonework and dusky Jacobean parlours—it had been an ancient Gilbertine monastery, secularized and altered after the Reformation—lay near the gently sloping banks of a river, amid the sleepy rural green of the Bedfordshire landscape, like a fragment of the past survived by chance into a later age. Day followed day there in eventless monotony, heavy with the memories of vanished days. Young though she was, Dorothy did not repine in such an atmosphere. It chimed with her prevailing mood. From her pale, well-bred countenance, framed by the dark ringlets and pearl eardrops of a Caroline lady, her heavy-lidded eyes looked out at the world—as they look out at us from her portrait still—with an expression of profound unostentatious sadness. Her eyes could not have looked sadder, so her mother used to tell her, if every friend she had in the world had died. And her demeanour was in keeping with her appearance. Strangers often found her formidable. Her manner was so reticent and "stately". She sat generally silent and abstracted in company, laughed very seldom, however uproarious the mirth around her, welcomed the departure of a visitor with hardly-concealed relief. This aloof gravity, however, was a deceptive mask. Beneath it quivered the flame of an exquisite responsiveness to life. In Dorothy Osborne, the society, of which she was a child, put forth its last fine flower. To something of her father's gallant nobility of temper, she joined a delicate Herrick-like sensibility. How she delighted to roam solitary by stream and pasture: she would sit absorbed for hours in a romance or a book of verses: her piety found its true echo in the melodious flowered pages of Jeremy Taylor. Above all her heart was imaginative; appreciative of every shade of intimacy and affection, and identifying itself so sensitively with other people's feelings that it was almost impossible for her to resist an appeal from anyone she loved. Yet there was nothing extravagant about her. Her taste was chastened by a vigilant sense of the value of dignity and restraint. Nothing disgusted her more for instance than to see a married couple too demonstrative to one another in public. Nor was she sentimental. Romantic though her feelings might be, they were checked at every turn by the judgments of her commonsense and her humour. For she had humour. The sad eyes could observe the world with a sharp-eyed amusement, that in the company of a sympathetic spirit, quickened to the bewitching mischief of a Rosalind. Indeed there is a lot of Rosalind about her—or is it Viola? Women like that actually did exist in that golden age: Shakespeare is a less unrealistic author than one might be inclined at times to suppose. Moreover, Dorothy had the Shakespearian natural-ness. Though she hated to give pain, it was impossible for her to say what she did not think. Even her shrewdness and her distinction had a naïve untaught freshness about them. The soft glow of poetry which trembles round her every move-ment exhales from her personality involuntarily, as the scent from a rose.

Alas, it was not time for roses to bloom. They shivered, they wilted in the wintry hurricane that was sweeping Eng-land. So sensitive a nature as Dorothy's was especially sus-ceptible to the shock of the contemporary catastrophe; and it attacked her at her most impressionable age. The break-up of her old home, the long miserable, poverty-stricken months of suspense at St. Malo, made still darker by the news of her brother's death, came on her during those early years before

the spirit has had time to grow a shell of philosophy or indifference, with which to withstand the blows of harsh
experience. She lost all her youthful spirits. "I was thought"
she says "as well-humoured an young person as most in
England; nothing dispirited, nothing troubled me. When I
came out of France nobody knew me again; I was so altered.
From a cheerful humour that was always alike, never over
merry, but always pleased, I was grown heavy and sullen,
froward and discomposed: and that country which usually gives
people a jollyness and gaiety that is natural to the climate, had
wraught in me so contrary effects, that I was as new a thing to
them as my clothes." Subsequent events had not been of a
kind to cheer her; the dismal years spent as a homeless refugee
in other people's houses, in an atmosphere loud with rumour
of battle and execution, and with the foundations of the world,
in which she had been brought up, crumbling around her;
then the return to a Chicksands, shorn of its former glory,
her father's decline, her mother's death. Not indeed that Lady
Osborne, embittered by years of misfortune, had been a
companion likely to brighten her daughter's view of life. By
nature Dorothy hated to think ill of people; but Lady Osborne
used to say to her "I have lived to see that it is almost
impossible to believe people worse than they are; and so
will you". Reluctantly, Dorothy began to fear she might be
right.

In fact, however, she had too generous a spirit to become a
misanthrope. All the same, experience had left an indelible
mark on her. Her gaiety had never come back. The brave
Elizabethan music was transposed into a minor key; Rosalind,
driven from Arden into a region of grim reality, had lost for
ever her sunshiny high-heartedness. And her adventurousness:
more tenaciously even than most of her contemporaries,
Dorothy clung to the security of established rule. Conventions
were an anchor of stability in an unstable universe. Besides,

those who broke them were objects of contempt and pity. Dorothy was obsessed by a nervous horror of being pitied: it was another effect of her misfortunes to intensify her sensitiveness to a morbid degree. This was why strangers found her manner so unforthcoming. The strain of her first encounter with the rough world had made her shrink from its contact: so that now she instinctively hid her true self behind the shield of an aloof formality. Her charm, her wit, became a secret treasure locked up in the cabinet of her reserve. But all this was symptomatic of a deeper injury. Calamity had undermined her fundamental confidence in life. Nothing was safe in the world she felt, man was not meant to be happy there. If he let himself believe he could be, so much the more dreadful would be his disappointment. This feeling was reinforced by the sterner elements in her creed. Did not Scripture teach her that the glories of this world were a snare and a delusion? Better then surely to withdraw from it; and, alone with her books and the meadows, in the twilight shelter of her old home, to dream away the days.

Dorothy might have resigned herself completely to such an existence but for one thing. So ardent and tender a temperament as hers was made for love: and already she had found it. In 1648 she and her youngest brother Robin, on their way to pay a visit to their father at St. Malo, found themselves delayed for a night or two, along with some other travellers, near Carisbrooke in the Isle of Wight, where Charles I was at that time lying imprisoned under the harsh guardianship of the Governor, Colonel Hammond. Robin Osborne's youthful cavalier blood boiled with indignation when he learned how his Royal Master was being treated. And, when the time came for them to continue their journey, he slipped away to scrawl a parting insult on a window-pane of the Inn. "Haman" it ran "was hanged on the gallows he had prepared for Mordecai." This was soon discovered: before they had gone far, messengers arrived to haul the impudent young malignant back to receive punishment. But when the party was led into the presence of Colonel Hammond, Dorothy sprang forward and said that it was she who had done it. On hearing this, Colonel Hammond allowed them to proceed. In those days even conscientious revolutionaries could be chivalrous. Still, it had been a brave act of Dorothy's: and it made a deep impression on one of her fellow travellers, a young man called Temple, who was journeying abroad in order to finish his education on the Continent. Already he had made her acquaintance: now, stirred by the romantic light in which she had shewn herself, he hastened to improve it. It cannot have been difficult for him. Lean and shapely, with beautiful curling hair falling on his shoulders, and a vivid, dark-eyed positive face agleam with intelligence, Temple's appearance was extremely prepossessing. And he had only to open his mouth to reveal himself as a fascinating talker, bubbling over with wit and fancy and bold entertaining opinions. Sea voyages are notoriously encouraging to intimacy. As the two young people sat talking on the deck of the little sailing ship, watching the changing spectacle of wave and cloud and fleeting glimpses of land, acquaintanceship warmed into friendship, friendship into something more. Love himself rose, like his mother, from the fresh sea foam, and, on footfall so soft that she was scarcely aware of it, stole into Dorothy's virgin heart. Temple's glowed with an answering fire. They arrived at St. Malo deeply committed to one another.

It was not to be wondered at. What man of taste could resist Dorothy if she allowed her charm to disclose its full sweetness? And Temple also, quite apart from his good looks, was exactly the type to attract her. William Temple had been born in 1628, the son and heir of Sir John Temple, Master of the Irish Rolls. In spite of the disturbances of the time, his education

had managed to follow the course thought suitable for a
gentleman. At school, Temple learnt to be an accomplished
classic; at Cambridge he explored the pleasures of social life
and played a lot of tennis. This versatility was typical of him.
His vivacious mind responded to almost every kind of
stimulus. Politics interested him intensely; so did Science,
History, the Arts, human nature in general. Interest stirred
him to thought. Incessantly he questioned, reflected, drew
conclusions. These were sometimes surprising. Temple had
all the clever young man's pleasure in opinions likely to shock
the conventional. Aristotle, in his view, had prostituted
Philosophy; and Queen Elizabeth, or "Bess Tidder" as he
preferred irreverently to call her, was a ridiculously over-rated
monarch, not to be mentioned in the same breath as Boadicea!
Indeed, young Temple was not a solid thinker. But he was
an enlivening one, sparkling with whim and spirit and personal idiosyncracy. "I never saw any sight, heard any sound . . .
but I could say I would rather have it continue or rather have it
cease" he notes. This fact about himself interested him.
Montaigne was one of his favourite authors; and he took a
Montaigne-like pleasure in examining his own mental processes. Why should he feel such a repulsion to tobacco, he
wondered, or to people with a stooping gait? Why should
he take for granted that any one woman called Arabella was
likely to be beautiful? Absorbed in such speculations, he would
sit for hours oblivious of the outside world following his train
of thought wherever it might lead him. "I know not what
'tis" he lamented ruefully, "that makes me so prone to the
posture of musing . . . what the French call reverie, a crowd
of restless capering antique fancies, bounding here and there,
fixing nowhere, building in one half hour castles in Ireland,
monasteries in France, palaces in Virginia, dancing at a
wedding, weeping at a burial, enthroned like a king, enragged
like a beggar, a lover, a friend, an indifferent person, and some-

times things of as little relation one with another as the Great Turk and a red-herring."

He was equally responsive to other kinds of pleasure—gambling, music, good wine, the charm of nature. "A fine day is a kind of sensual pleasure" he once said. Yet, there was nothing unbridled about his enjoyment. Always he was restrained by a natural moral fastidiousness, an innate temperance of taste. Indeed, though none of his talents were of the first order, he had the judgment and the sense of style to make the very most of them. Already, at twenty-one, he was a brilliant example of the Caroline ideal of a gentleman, in whom every element of the good life, moral, intellectual, and physical, were blended together in a cool harmony.

He had the weaknesses of his type though. Pride for instance: Temple could not endure taking orders from anyone, and so disliked being under an obligation that, if he was given a present, he was uneasy till he had sent back a better one. His sensitiveness too, could be altogether too much of a good thing. In later life he refused to spend even a night in London, he thought it smelt so disagreeable; damp weather produced in him a fit of nervous depression. He could not stand being kept waiting, loathed the sound of church bells, lost his temper in an argument, had no patience with a fool. When a young man told him that he thought Montaigne like St. Augustine—it certainly was a silly remark—Temple simply turned his back on him. Even with those he loved he could be extremely difficult; sometimes sunk in a black gloom in which he would scarcely speak, at other moments protesting violently that they did not respond to him with the ardour that such an affection as his deserved.

Indeed he had something of the egotism and all of the arrogance of the brilliant young man he was. In consequence, more commonplace people did not take to him. They thought his manners conceited, and suspected the mocking tone of his conversation. Most likely he was at heart a rebel and an atheist. These last two accusations were unjustified. His aristocratic tastes and temperament combined to make Temple a steady supporter of Church and King. But it is true that he was in strong reaction against the fanatical partisanship which had animated the previous generation. He had seen too much of its unpleasant fruits at home. Sir John Temple— a less heroic spirit than Sir Peter Osborne—had striven to drive a middle course in the political and religious struggle; with the result that he had quarrelled first with the Court and then with Cromwell, who in 1648 had dismissed him from his offices. His son had grown up disgusted with extremism in any form, sceptical of any kind of enthusiasm, in favour of any policy which seemed likely to make things work smoothly and tranquilly, and with a premature realization of the stable concrete satisfactions of existence. "What do you wish for most in the world?" a friend once asked him. "Health, peace, and fair weather" replied the youthful Temple. Now and again, if his mind chanced on some scheme which he thought might solve a political problem, he felt an impulse to fling himself into the mêlée. But most of the time he yearned for a life of civilized retirement in which he could cultivate the pleasures of mind, and senses, and observe with smiling detachment the humours of mankind.

He had Dorothy with him here. He had Dorothy with him everywhere. It was not only that he must have been far more attractive and intelligent than the other young men she had met. At last amid the thronging hordes of a humanity immersed in practical business and political conflict, her eyes had met those of a kindred spirit; someone who set the same supreme value, as she did, on reading and the country and intimacy and contemplation. More important, he fortified her where she was weakest. For it was not in Temple to be pessimistic— at least not for long. He refused to believe that man was intended to be unhappy. If circumstances were untoward, circumstances could and must be altered.. In the presence of his sanguine vitality, Dorothy felt her old lost confidence in living, stealing deliciously back. There is no affinity more perfect than that founded on similar tastes and complimentary temperaments. Even Temple's weaknesses appealed to her, his intolerance, his wilfulness. She recognized them as wrong, but she liked him all the better for being wrong in that sort of way. The very fact that Dorothy's feelings, naturally so ardent, had for so long been frustrated by her fear of life, made her yield herself all the more completely once her defences were broken down. Her heart was Temple's for ever, even if fate should decide they were never to be united.

By 1652 it looked sadly probable that this was fate's decision. It was a difficult time to get married in any circumstances, with the order of life uprooted and everyone scattered and impoverished. In wistful day-dream Dorothy pictured herself and Temple stealing away to some remote place, perhaps the little island of Herm which they had passed, lying serene and forgotten in the ocean, on their voyage out; there to dwell safe from the injuries of the world. "Do you remember Herm and the little house there?" she was to write to him later; "Shall we go thither? that is next to being out of the world: there we might live like Baucis and Philemon and grow old together, and for our charity to some shipwrackt stranger, obtain the blessing of both dying at the same time. How idly I talk! 'tis because the story please me, none in Ovid so much. I remember I cried when I read it. Methought they were the perfectest character of a contented marriage, where piety and love were all their world." It was not only the world that stood between Dorothy and a contented marriage. In those days marriage was looked on as a social arrangement, in which the approval of the family counted for far more than the inclinations of the parties. Both families were against this

19

match. Why they were so strongly against it is a little obscure:
as usual in those days, money seems to have been the trouble.
The Osbornes thought that Dorothy would be throwing
herself away on a suitor with no better financial prospects than
Temple; while Sir John Temple considered that an accomplished young man like his son had a right to expect a more
splendid fortune than Dorothy could offer. It was he who
first put his foot down. After arriving at St. Malo, Temple
had lingered on there for a month or two to enjoy Dorothy's
society. Suddenly he got a message from his father, who had
somehow got news of his entanglement, peremptorily com-
manding him to leave at once for Paris in order to pursue the
education for which he had been sent abroad. Reluctantly the
lovers said farewell; it was two years before they saw each
other again.

Themselves they did not look on this farewell as final.
There was no question indeed—even in their own minds—of
defying the family ban. But they still hoped that, if they
waited, fortune might change. Meanwhile, the separation was
pretty complete. Dorothy was soon settled at Chicksands,
while Temple roamed about France and the low countries.
Owing to distance and to family disapproval they could only
manage to write very rarely. Temple almost wished it was
never, so exasperating did he find the suspense when he did
expect a letter from Dorothy and it failed to come. To his
high-strung, uncontrolled temperament the whole situation
was a dreadful strain. He found it equally hard to sleep at night
or to get up in the morning; and lay abed for hours railing at
fortune, and analyzing his state of mind. To distract himself,
he started adapting into English some French love stories.
The task occupied his sleepless hours, and the translation of his
heroes' amorous speeches provided an outlet for his pent-up
emotions. "I send you these stories" he writes in a dedication
to Dorothy, "whose rememberance indited whatever is

passionately said in any line of them." As an additional relief
to his feelings, he interspersed the narrative with cutting comments on the crass stupidity of parents who pretend to understand their children's dispositions.

In 1651 he returned to his country, but not to peace of mind.
Impossible as it was for him to visit Chicksands, he was almost
as cut off from Dorothy as he had been on the Continent: and
the strain on his nerves was aggravated by the fact that his
father was always worrying him with proposals to marry him
to other ladies. William passed his time as best he could,
talking and writing in London, or staying at his friend
Richard Franklyn's place at Moor Park, whose stately garden,
with its grottoes and plashing fountains, and leafy balustrated
vistas, did something to soothe his unquiet spirit. One day
there, looking out of the window, his eye was caught by a
statue of Leda, gazing in classic and eternal repose across the
terraced sward. Moved by a fanciful impulse, he wrote with a
diamond on the pane:

> "Tell me Leda which is best
> Ne'er to move or ne'er to rest.
> Speak that I may know thereby
> Who is happier thou or I."

Towards the end of the summer, Dorothy contrived some
pretext to come to London; and at last they met. But again
Sir John Temple got wind of it. Summoning William to
York, where he was then living, he ordered him to go on his
travels once more.

Our information about William during the period that
followed this second disappointment is tantalizingly scanty.
But it looks as if, under its shock, his hopes had begun to flag;
and with them, his determination. The very impulsiveness of
his temperament made him ill-equipped to stand the ordeal of

an indefinitely long frustration. He still wrote for his pleasure; but instead of love romances, his literary efforts now consist of reflections on topics suggested by his life abroad; the character of the Archduke Leopold, the influence of chance on politics, the languages of Flanders and Germany. These last did not please him. "The Almane" he says "is a language I should never learn unless 'twas to fright children when they cried; yet methinks it should be good to clear a man's throat that was hoarse with a cold. I have heard some speak it so as they have made me expect the words should break down their teeth as they rushed out of their mouth. . . . Flemish is a lower, yet to my mind a worse sound. I could never esteem a lady handsome whilst she spoke it; and I believe the ladies are generally conscious of it, for in company none of them will ever speak it. The tone is the more displeasing because it sounds as if those who spoke it were displeased and seeming arrogant withal. They talk as if a man owed them money and would not pay them." In spite of their unmelodious tongue, however, he liked the Flemish well enough to contemplate settling in their country permanently. Meanwhile, he only wrote to Dorothy once in a year: and, when in the Autumn of 1652, he paid another visit to England, he took no step to get into touch with her.

She for her part had also begun to relinquish hope. Though she was more patient by nature than Temple, she was also far more easily disheartened. Moreover, it was harder for her to put up a fight. Even more than men, women were expected then to bow to the will of their relations in affairs of the heart: they were hardly supposed to admit to themselves that they felt an affection unless they knew it would be approved. After Dorothy got back to England, suitors began to appear: and her family, taking for granted that all was over between her and Temple, opened negotiations with them. Luckily these fell through. But, while they were on, Dorothy, though she raised every objection she could, had to behave as though she were perfectly ready to entertain any really eligible offer. Indeed, she was far too sensible not to realize that whatever her feelings for Temple, she might in the end have to resign herself to marrying someone else. Such marriages, were, after all, the common way of the world. The difficulty of her situation began to tell on her nerves. Temple's second departure plunged her into a morbid melancholy. She was consumed by a superstitious fear that she was destined never to see him again. His subsequent silence intensified this fear. The long, empty days at Chicksands spent brooding on the unpromising future reduced her to such a state of nervous depression that her family noticed it and took her for a cure to the waters of Epsom. By the winter she was calm again, but not more hopeful. After three years waiting, her union with Temple seemed further off than ever. Family opposition had not grown less; and now perhaps Temple himself was sheering off. Dorothy was the more disposed to be impressed by these facts because they chimed with her temperamental despondency. The course of her love story had only served to confirm her conviction that it was no use her looking to this life for happiness. "I do not know" she wrote "that I ever desired anything earnestly in my life but 'twas denied me; I am many times afraid to wish a thing, merely lest that my fortune should take that occasion to use me ill." She could not help still cherishing Temple's image in her heart; but she had made up her mind that she had better give up thinking that she was ever likely to marry him.

Then, in December, he wrote her a letter. It had not turned out so easily for a discriminating young man to forget Dorothy Osborne; now that he was within reach of her, the dwindling flame of his passion had begun to burn up afresh. She wrote back at once. In this reply Dorothy makes her first personal appearance on the stage of recorded history; for the first time we hear her voice.

Its accents are not those of a lover. Till she knew what he really felt, pride forbade her to commit herself. Besides, she was too tactful. What could be more foolish than to adopt a tone that would be embarrassing to both of them if, as was only too likely, the relationship between them was destined to grow no closer. Temple's letter, we gather, was a light tentative affair, designed to discover whether she was willing to reopen the relationship. Long ago he had laughingly bet her ten pounds that she would be married before they met again. Now he asked her if he owed her the money. Her reply is a little masterpiece in the art of handling a delicate situation. No, she says in the easy tones of old friendship, he did not owe her the ten pounds: yes, she was extremely glad to hear from him. And then at the end, consciously or not, she allows just a hint of her warmer interest to betray itself.

"To find that you have overcome your long journey, that you are well, and in a place where it is possible for me to see you, is such a satisfaction as I, who have not been used to many, may be allowed to doubt of. Yet I will hope my eyes do not deceive me and that I have not forgot to read. But if you please to confirm it to me by another, you know how to direct it; for I am where I was, still the same, and always

yours humble servant,
Dorothy Osborne."

This gave him an opening; but not too obviously. If he should not choose to follow it up no harm was done. However he did. By return of post came a request to know what had happened to her. And soon they were exchanging long letters into which they poured all the chronicle of their life and feelings during the period of separation. Dorothy's tone, however, though intimate and evidently out to please, was still carefully not serious. If she says an affectionate thing, it is half flippantly. Temple's inflammable spirit began to chafe at this: he was also disturbed by her references to other suitors. What did she mean by them? He demanded that she should declare her feelings to him more ardently, or, as he put it "more kindly". At this, Dorothy, gaily, but firmly, pulled him up. What reason had he to distrust the sincerity of an old friend like herself? It was he who was unkind to complain. And a little later, she lets fall a remark reminding him demurely that he had given her reason to be cautious. "I have foresworn being deceived twice by the same person" said she. No—till Dorothy was quite sure of her position she was not going to be drawn, protest Temple as loudly as he liked. He did not have to protest long. Early in February Dorothy went to London for ten days, and Temple got a note from her: "This is to tell you that you will be expected about nine o'clock at a lodging over against the place where Charing Cross stood, and two doors above the Goat Tavern. If with this direction you can find it out, you will find one that is very much your servant." Beyond the fact that they enjoyed a good laugh together listening to the agitated prophesyings of an Anabaptist preacher, there is no record of what passed between them during Dorothy's sojourn in the capital. But her letters, after she got home, reveal that the meeting had been enough to set her doubts at rest. Once in each other's presence it had been clear that the years of separation had made no difference to their sentiment for one another. No longer does Dorothy make any secret of her feelings; and, though she still talks airily of her suitors, and even proposes herself to find a wife for Temple, there is now no doubt that this is all a joke. The practical obstacles to their marriage might seem as insurmountable as ever. But each was sure of the other; and this made all the difference. Once more they settled down hopefully to wait. Meanwhile they alleviated the pains of absence by means of a regular correspondence.

It was conducted under certain difficulties. On Monday Dorothy's letter left for London by carrier; and, perhaps because she did not wish her family to know how often she wrote to Temple, Dorothy directed it under cover to a Mrs. Painter in Covent Garden, whence the carrier fetched Temple's answer early on Thursday. Much too early, grumbled Temple, who, if he had not managed to get his letter off in good time, had to get up at four o'clock in the morning in order to catch the post. Dorothy teased him about the dreadful way she interfered with his most cherished habits. Still, we need not pity him too much; the effort must have been worth it. For it is now that Dorothy's talent as a letter writer gets into its stride. The window which she opens for us into seventeenth century England swings wide; and for a year we watch, week by week and at the closest quarters, the movement of her thought and mood, and the manner of her life.

It was a confined sort of life. In those days it was considered impossible for an unmarried girl of good family to travel alone. Before she could move, therefore, Dorothy had to wait till she could find someone, preferably a relation, who happened to be travelling and could act as chaperone. The gentry of England were for the most part living in such a quiet way that Dorothy's relations seldom found occasion to travel. Soon an event took place which further limited her opportunities for moving. Sir Peter Osborne, attending service at his private chapel on Easter Sunday, was suddenly taken very ill. After a week or two spent hanging between life and death, he recovered from this particular attack. But under its shock, his already weakened health finally gave way. From this time on he was an invalid and never left his room. Somebody had to look after him: and since none of his other children lived at home regularly, this somebody was inevitably Dorothy. For eight months she never left Chicksands. She was not without companions, however. A gentleman's

household in the seventeenth century was still feudal enough
to be a community of which master and servant alike felt
themselves a living member. Although Dorothy's servants
regarded her no doubt as a being of a superior order, she was
on personal terms with them. And the simplicity of living,
which mingled so strangely with the formality of that world,
made these terms easy and intimate. At the crisis of her father's
illness she sat up night after night watching by his bedside,
with his manservant—"a poor moping creature" said Dorothy
—who she had to keep on talking to in order to stop him
dropping off to sleep. To refresh them a maid would bring
up a bottle of ale. And then, by the light of a candle shaded
from where, in the dim recesses of the sick-chamber, the old
Knight dozed in his curtained four-poster, all three would
drink together. The Chicksands household had also its
superior dependents—the clergyman, the bailiff, and their
families—who formed, as it were, a little court round the
monarchs of the great house which was the centre of their
existence. The daughter of Sir Peter Osborne's old bailiff, a
Miss Jane Wright, actually lived at Chicksands for a time;
where she acted as a sort of lady-in-waiting, Nerissa to
Dorothy's Portia. She talked to guests if Dorothy felt disinclined; she helped to preserve the proprieties by staying in a
room when a gentleman called; she helped Dorothy to get
exercise in wet weather by playing battledore and shuttlecock
with her. Above all, she was valuable as a confidant. Jane
Wright seems to have been the only person in the secret of
Dorothy's romance. Temple got to know her; and when she
left to go to London she brought him the latest news of his
love.

Dorothy's solitude was also qualified by an occasional
visitor. These were always relations; her brothers, her
brother-in-law Sir Thomas Peyton and his daughter, her
cousins Mrs. Thorold and Mr. Molle. Dorothy did not enjoy

having these last two to stay. Cousin Molle was a pompous fussy, Cambridge don, preposterously proud of his pedantic style of letter-writing, and so exercised about his health that Dorothy came to the conclusion he preferred being ill, since only then had he the excuse to cosset himself as much as he wanted. This hypochondria, however, was sometimes a godsend. Once, seized by a fancy that he had got dropsy, cousin Molle cut his visit short in the middle in order to hurry off panic-stricken to Cambridge to see his doctor. The widow Thorold was equally trying. Two days of her incessant conversation was enough to leave Dorothy prostrate with boredom; even though she had played cards with her by the hour, regardless of how much money she herself might lose, in order to check its flow. Compared with the widow, her niece Miss Peyton—"a girl sent into the world" says her aunt "in order to show that 'tis possible for a woman to be silent"—must have been a relief. Dorothy found her a sympathetic spirit in other ways. Shy and pensive, Miss Peyton appreciated the melancholy charm of Chicksands, where she liked to wander in the woods for hours, collecting mosses. She was also agreeably pretty. "If I had any desire to gain a servant" remarked Dorothy archly—"I should not like her company."

As it happened, Dorothy—apart from the fact that she was by nature singularly free from feminine jealousy—was, in her present circumstances, anxious to check, rather than to encourage male attentions. Her suitors, or "servants" as she called them, were the chief bane of her existence. For two years now hardly a month had passed without a new one appearing: and there seemed no reason to suppose that the unwelcome procession would ever stop. They were very varied. The greatest catch among them was Henry Cromwell, second son of the Protector. It is a measure of the relative mildness of temper in which the Civil War was conducted that neither Cromwells nor Osbornes seemed to have objected to such an alliance.

Henry Cromwell indeed was very different from his formidable father; shockingly different, strict puritans lamented. A
cheerful, convivial, sporting young gentleman, he wooed
Dorothy with presents of greyhounds. Though she liked
greyhounds, Dorothy found nothing in him to incline her to
weaken. Nor in her cousin Thomas Osborne, afterwards the
famous Lord Danby. Other people might think him handsome, she did not: besides, he told lies, and had an interfering
mother. If these suitors failed to move her, she was not likely
to yield to a dumb young man with whom she had to converse
by signs and grimaces. "I wonder people live, who have to do
so" she exclaimed.

Young gentlemen, however, whether dumb or talkative,
were exceptional among Dorothy's wooers. Her dignified
demeanour and reputation for discretion made her an especial
magnet for middle-aged men anxious to get married, but nervous lest too youthfully exuberant a bride might disturb the
staid harmony of their existence. There was Mr. Bennett, the
High Sheriff of Cambridgeshire, there was Mr. Wingfield—
"a modest, melancholy, reserved man" observed Dorothy
"whose heart is so taken up with little philosophical studies
that I wonder how I found a room there". Above all, there
was Sir Justinian Isham. Sir Justinian was the most importu-
nate of her suitors. Rich, learned, reputed to be a pattern
of wisdom, and highly respected in Northamptonshire, he
had entered on to the scene two years before with such a con-
quering flourish of trumpets that Dorothy wondered what
possible excuse she should ever find for rejecting him. To her
mingled amusement and relief, however, Sir Justinian, or
"the Emperor" as she irreverently called him, turned out to be
not up to his reputation. "'Twas the vainest impertinent, self-
conceited, learned cockscomb that ever I saw", said she. An
elderly widower with four depressed grown-up daughters,
whom he kept immured in his gloomy house in Nottingham-

shire, he expressed himself in a jargon of fantastic pomposity, and was so vain that he warned Dorothy that he had been forced to keep his attentions to her a secret, lest they should arouse the jealousy of the magnificent Lady Sunderland. Dorothy managed to put him off the first time he proposed: but, after fruitlessly trying the effect of his charms on six other ladies, he returned to the attack; explaining, surprisingly, that he was sure there was a peculiar affinity between himself and Dorothy, because, shortly after hearing that she was suffering from an ague, he had contracted one himself.

Altogether, Dorothy's opinion of mankind was not raised by her suitors. If they had done nothing else for her, they had taught her what she did not want in a husband. As a relief to her feelings she expatiated on this topic to Temple.

"He should not be so much a country gentleman as to understand nothing but hawks and dogs, and to be fonder of either than of his wife; nor of the next sort of them, whose aim reaches no further than to be Justice of Peace, and once in his life High Sheriff, who read no book but Statutes and studies nothing but how to make a speech inter-larded with Latin, that may amaze his disagreeing poor neighbours, and fright them rather than persuade them into quietness. He must not be a thing that began the world in a free school, was sent from thence to the University, and is at his farthest when he reaches the Inns of Court; has no acquaintance but those of his form in these places, speaks the French he has picked out of old laws, and admires nothing but the stories he has heard of the revels that were kept there before his time. He must not be a Town-gallant neither, that lives in a tavern and an ordinary, that cannot imagine how an hour should be spent without company, unless it be in sleeping, that makes court to all the women he sees, thinks they believe him, and is laughed at equally. Nor a travelled monsieur whose head is all feather inside and outside; that can talk of nothing but dances and duels, and has courage enough to wear slashes when everybody else dies with cold to see him. He must not be a fool of no sort, nor peevish ill-natured, nor proud nor covetous, and to all this must be added 'he must love me'."

These spirited portraits were drawn from her neighbours as well as her suitors. Dorothy saw a certain amount of the neighbours: for, though the disturbances of the time had diminished the social life of the country gentry, it had not upset the structure of society so much as to stop it altogether. On occasions of official festivity, like Christmas, people still climbed into their coaches to jolt over the cart-tracks they called roads, in order to consume a heavy dinner together. Married couples and recent arrivals to the district still paid and received visits of ceremony. County society was no more brilliant then than it is now; certainly not so brilliant as to lure Dorothy from her shell. For the most part she found these entertainments a burden. Still, they had their compensations. It was delightful to get the chance to look at beautiful Lady Grey de Ruthin for example; or to talk over the news with charming, intelligent Lady Diana Rich. Though Dorothy preferred living out of the great world, she was always interested to hear about it. Now, especially, when she was buried down at Chicksands, she drank up every item of information. Sometimes the news was political. With ironical amusement Dorothy heard of the difficulties overtaking the revolutionary government. Cromwell's expulsion of the Parliament, for example; what would Mr. Pym have said, she wondered, had he lived to see this consequence of the victory of the so-called party of freedom. No doubt such speculations were treasonable, she commented sarcastically; she had better check them. She was also entertained that people should be so shocked at General Monk marrying a seamstress. Surely she was no more unsuitable to her position than the rest of the Parliamentary ladies. For the most part, however, Dorothy kept off politics. They reminded her too painfully of what she longed to forget. For the dark cloud of death and defeat still brooded, ominous and unbroken over the landscape of the private scene. If one raised one's eyes there it was, casting a shadow over the spirit. Nearly every family of her acquaintance had its tragedy. Lady Diana Rich's father had been executed; so had Lady Ann Wentworth's. Dorothy heard that Mr. Waller, the poet, was writing a romance about the recent war. "If he does not mingle it with a great deal of pleasing fiction, it cannot be very diverting, sure" she said "the subject is so sad."

There was nothing sad about social news, however. Dorothy enjoyed this thoroughly. The scandals and the vagaries of the Caroline aristocracy dance their way through her pages, blending strangely with the melancholy of her reflections on life and the sweetness of her words of love. Fancy Lady Isabella Thynne marrying a man "no better than a beast, only because he had a great estate"; or Miss de Mayerne falling in love with "a buffle-headed French Marquis" and kissing him publicly in the Park too; or Lord Leicester quarrelling with his wife after forty years of tranquil marriage, and dismissing all the servants just to spite her; or the fantastic Lady Newcastle publishing a book of verses! "They say 'tis ten times more extravagant than her dress", said Dorothy; and, when she had read it, "I am satisfied there are many soberer people in Bedlam".

News and visitors, however, were only an occasional interruption in her sequestered existence. Indeed, though they might entertain her for a moment, they only ruffled the surface of her attention. During the long hours she spent alone she thought little about them; and these were the hours she valued most. Throughout the cold spring months, she escaped from company whenever she could to muse with a book over the fire; or, when the days warmed and lengthened, to wander in the countryside. Summer weather quickened her feelings to a peculiar intensity. Living as they did far closer to the primitive earth than we do, the Carolines were far more affected by its moods. How untiringly and with what an unfailingly responsive zest do their poets harp on the changes of the seasons; green Spring, Summer with its July flowers, the rich fecundity of Autumn. The cold dark Winter months, spent in those unheated houses, chilled and darkened the hearts of their inhabitants. At the turn of the year, when the buds broke and the birds began to sing and build, their spirits too bloomed and carolled in sympathy. Dorothy has left us a record of a typical summer day at Chicksands. She rose early, and after seeing to the household, stepped out into the garden to taste the morning freshness. When it grew too hot—they seem to have been strangely sensitive to heat in those days—she went in to pay a visit to Sir Peter lying always immobile in his bedroom before settling down to array herself in all the elaboration of Caroline full dress. Next came dinner, conducted—even if she were alone or with a single guest—with formal ceremony in the great dining-room. The afternoon was spent in retirement reading or sewing. Then, when the fierceness of the day's heat had begun to abate, she went out once more. "About six or seven o'clock I walk out into a common that lies hard by the house, where a great many young wenches keep sheep and cows and sit in the shade singing ballads. I go to them and compare their voices and beauties to some ancient shepherdesses that I have read of, and find a vast difference there. But, trust me, I think these are as innocent as those could be. I talk to them and find they want nothing to make them the happiest people in the world but the knowledge that they are so. Most commonly, when we

33

are in the midst of our discourse, one looks about her and spies
a cow going into the corn, and away they all run as if they had
wings at their heels. I that am not so nimble stay behind, and,
when I see them driving home their cattle, I think 'tis time for
me to retire too." Supper followed; and after supper back
into the open air where, amid the fading twilight, sweet with
the vagrant scents of a country evening, she would stroll in
the garden or sit by the banks of the stream, dreaming—of
Temple and love undying and hope deferred—while time
slipped by unnoticed, till suddenly she looked up and it was
night and she must steal back into the silence of the sleeping
house, and, candle in hand, climb the shadowy staircase to
bed.

The current of her meditations was coloured by her reading.
Dorothy read enormously, anything she could lay hands on,
poetry, travels, devotional works, romances. Romances were
what she liked best. It seems odd that it should have been so;
for the romances of that age are, to our eyes, very tedious
affairs; incredible, interminable tales, couched in a style of
stilted rhetoric about Amestris and Aglatides, Artibis and
Cleobuline, kings and princesses of preposterous beauty and
virtue, who strut their way, volume after volume, through a
monotonous labyrinth of improbable intrigue, conventional
sentiment, and far-fetched punctilios of honour. Dorothy,
however, discussed their characters as seriously as we should
discuss that of Anna Karenina, cried over their troubles, and
was so enthralled by their adventures that she would sit up
reading, night after night, long after she should have been in
bed. Like the rest of her contemporaries, she was accustomed
to rhetoric, and found no difficulty in believing the improbable. Besides, the subject of these romances was love. And love
was to Dorothy the most interesting subject in the world.

How should it have been otherwise! In the radiant warmth
of her re-union with Temple, the flower of her passion had

opened wide, so that it now diffused its invisible perfume over
her every mood and thought. "My very dreams are yours",
she cries to him. Wherever she was and whatever she was
doing—gazing at the shepherdesses, topicing with cousin
Molle, drowsily watching by her father's bedside in the silence
of the night—the figure of Temple floated before her mental
eye, obscuring the outside world. She grew more abstracted
than ever. One evening, seated by the fire in company with
her brother and a friend of his, lost in her own thoughts, she
found her attention suddenly seized by their conversation.
They were talking about flying. Ah! If she could cover the
distance between herself and Temple with such an airy swift-
ness! To their amused surprise Dorothy suddenly broke
silence, demanding excitedly if flying was really going to be
possible. Nor did love only increase her absent-mindedness.
The arrival of the post, for instance, agitated her so violently
as to make her for the time being quite unlike her usual controlled self. She would shout to the maid, calling her in the
dim dawn, to tear open the curtains in order that she might
see if any of the letters, that had come to her, were from
Temple; she would drop her hand in the middle of a game ot
cards because she heard a courier from London riding by; and
she would stand in the mud and straw of the stable exasper-
atedly upbraiding the groom for daring to unharness his horse
before opening the letter bag. When they did come, Temple's
letters never seemed long enough for her. "If you do not send
me long letters, then you are the cruellest person that can be.
If you love me you will, and, if you do not, I shall never love
myself."

Interest in her own love-story led her to speculate on the
subject of love in general. In this she was the child of her age.
It is hardly to be supposed that the Carolines felt the passion of
love more intensely than we do; but certainly they thought
about it much more. Four-fifths of their poetry is love-

poetry; and their prose too is largely devoted to celebrating its glories, analysing its nature and cataloguing its varieties. The fact that they were an aristocratic society accounts partly for this preoccupation. Alas, it is only people, untroubled by the necessity of making a living, who have the leisure and energy to study their sentiments with this elaborate refinement. But in the Carolines, natural tendency was encouraged by their ideal mode of thought. If love was a worthy passion, then it had to be fitted into their general philosophical scheme, and its relation to the principle of virtue must be discovered and defined. Further, believing in form as they did, they were interested to decide the correct mode for love's expression. How should a lover speak and dress and behave himself in the presence of his mistress, they asked themselves. With what appropriate graces should he adorn the utterance of his heart? At once a faith and a fine art, love was to them a necessary element of the good life, and as such required intensive study.

Yet their view of it was not the same as that of latter-day amorists. Nowhere does their peculiar blend of realism and romance appear more conspicuously. In some ways it was a highly romantic view. Did they not see in the affinity of two noble spirits a symbol and revelation of the divine harmony of the universe, and in the lover's desire for the beloved an expression of the desire of the soul for perfection? But they did not think, in the Byronic fashion, that love had a right to override every other consideration in order to achieve its fulfilment. On the contrary, the very fact that they considered it a necessary element of the good life meant that it must not be permitted to clash with its other elements. At every turn passion must take account of the obligations of religion, of man's duty to society and his family. Dorothy's conviction of the value of convention made her especially conscious of these obligations. For although love meant so much to her, she thought it should be kept on a tight rein. Unbridled passion was always wrong, above all, in women. A woman must be sure her love was requited before she yielded to it, much less confess it to the man of her choice. Even then she should make sure that it was a rational passion, founded on esteem for his character. Apart from anything else, what she had seen of the world had taught Dorothy that unless it was so founded, it would soon evaporate. "When there is no reason to uphold a passion", she notes, "it will sink of itself."

"But", she goes on "when there is, it may last eternally." If all the conditions were satisfied, if it was grounded on regard and ruled by principle, then Dorothy conceived of love with all the enthusiastic elevation of her age. True love was the expression of a complete and unique harmony between two minds and hearts. An equal harmony too; for, though for form's sake, lovers might speak of one another as mistress and servant, in relation to their love they were free and equal partners. How contemptibly mistaken a view of the subject did it reveal in Lady Sunderland, that she should say that she had given her heart to Mr. Smith only out of pity for his passion for her. Then, true love implied complete confidence. If each lover was genuinely the other's affinity, there could be no reason for tactful concealments, let alone for jealousy. The franker lovers were, the more fully would the harmony between them appear, and both must realize that no one else could ever supply the other's place. Indeed, this realization was a primary condition of true love. Dorothy could never, she said, believe in the homage of a heart that had been offered to another. So monogamous a conception of love could only find its true fulfilment in marriage. As a matter of fact, Dorothy's religious principles were far too strict for her to try and imagine it on any other terms.

On the other hand, she was forced only too often to imagine marriage without love. Like everyone else in the seventeenth century, Dorothy accepted the view that marriage was a social institution not necessarily entered upon for sentimental reasons. This meant that it had its own problems unconnected with those of the heart. These also Dorothy found extremely interesting. Next to love, marriage—its demands and duties and difficulties—was the main subject of her hours of reflection. Here once more her moral principles combined with commonsense to decide her notions. Rank and money were solid goods—Dorothy was far too clear-sighted not to recognize this—but they were insufficient in themselves to make a good marriage. A woman was not justified in marrying a man she did not respect unless divine authority, in the shape of her parents, absolutely ordered her to do so. But if they did so order, or if she found she had been deceived as to her husband's character—what then? Then, said Dorothy, she must patiently make the best of it. She thought it dreadful for a woman to bully her husband: and, with a slightly bitter smile she praises the discretion of a lady she knew, who, married to a man whose disturbing habit it was suddenly to get up in the middle of the night and beat a table with a stick, made no protest; but took care to put a cushion on the table before she went to bed. It was the woman's rôle to submit to the man: and generally her fault, so Dorothy had noted, if a marriage failed to go smoothly. All the same, Dorothy could not approve of La Reine Margot being so easy-going about her husband's infidelities. A woman must keep her dignity. This concern for dignity made Dorothy oddly severe on anyone who married a second time. They could only do it for worldly advantages, or out of uncontrolled physical passion. Both motives were ignoble. She also thought it ignoble for a woman to try and rule her husband by wheedling and flattery. She herself could never stoop to do it. But indeed, when she came to consider her own case, she did not see how she could make a success of marriage to anyone she cared for less than she cared for Temple. It was nothing to be proud of. Simply she found it too difficult to subdue her will and hide her true feelings. Still, perhaps she was not alone in this. For as far as she could see most marriages were unhappy; and most couples if they had been able to live together for a year before marrying, would have broken off their engagement. In marriage, as in every other human institution—so ran Dorothy's characteristic conclusion—things seemed likely to turn out badly.

Such was the scene, such the preoccupations mirrored in the pages that, traceried over in Dorothy's delicate, precise hand, found their way each Thursday morning on to Temple's writing table. Her handwriting was a work of art: so were her letters. In addition to their historical and personal interest, they were exquisite pieces of literature. Not that they give the effect of conscious art. Indeed, half the charm of Dorothy's letters comes from the fact that she seems to be just writing whatever comes into her head, without any eye to the impression she is making; mingling grave and gay, turning from a declaration of love to Lady Newcastle's oddities, from Lady Newcastle's oddities to a practical request—will Temple go to the Royal Exchange and order some orange flower water for her, or can he get her one of the new fashionable engraved seals—and then from a practical request to a reflection on the vanity of human wishes. Her style seems as unstudied as her matter. Dorothy was strongly of the opinion that any other sort of style was unsuitable for letters. "All letters methinks should be free and easy as one's discourse, not studied as an oration, nor made up of hard words like a charm. 'Tis an admirable thing to see how some people will labour to find out terms that may obscure a plain sense; like a gentleman, I knew, who would never say 'the weather grew cold', but that 'winter began to salute us'. I have no patience for such coxcombs."

Her practice followed her precept. The language of her letters is colloquial; the tone intimate and easy. She exclaims, interrupts herself, breaks off—just as if she were talking. We seem less to read her letters than to overhear them. Here it is, though, that her art lies. It is not easy to get the sound of the voice into the written word. Spontaneous though she wanted her letters to appear, in fact Dorothy selected and arranged her matter; so that her every sentence contributed to bring her personality breathing and alive on to the page. Further, she had a natural artist's sense of style, which led her always to try and present her thoughts in a delightful form. The simple word is the right word; and the movement of her sentences, whether lightly dancing or slowing down to a grave andante, or swelling out in the lingering interweaving cadences of seventeenth-century eloquence, is always the clear echo to the movement of her mood and thought. Nor, for all her intimacy, is she ever vulgarly informal. That curious blend of naïveté and ceremoniousness, which characterized her period, was so bred in her bone that even at her most natural, she instinctively preserves a charming courtliness. Her exclamations and interruptions are never abrupt. She always remembers to end her briefest note with a turn of finished grace:

"Chide me when I do anything that is not well; but then make haste to tell me that you forgive me, and that you are, as I shall ever be,

A faithful friend
Dorothy Osborne."

Indeed, Dorothy was too unself-conscious to be shy of saying something pretty, if it was needed to convey her meaning. This was a great help to her when it came to writing love-letters. The love-letters of more self-conscious ages make depressing reading. Their shame-faced slangy endearments sound both flat and embarrassing. Passion needs the restraint of a formalized mode of utterance, to give it shape and to crystallize its intensity. No one ever wrote better love-letters than stately Dorothy. There are few endearments in them, and no rhapsodies. But even when she is telling the news, or asking Temple to do some commission for her, the emotion that filled her heart vibrates through every modulation of her voice; and now it gleams out in an enchanting playfulness; and now, as a wave of passionate longing for Temple floods over her, it flows forth in a strain of tenderness, all the more poignant for the delicate reticence with which it is expressed. "You are as much pleased, you say, in writing to me, as I can be to receive your letters. Why should not you think the same of me? In earnest you may; and if you love me, you will. But then, how much more satisfied should I be if there were no need of these; and we might talk all that we write and more. Shall we ever be so happy? Last night I was in the garden until 11 o'clock. It was the sweetest night that e'er I saw, the garden looked so well, and the jessamine smelt beyond all perfume: and yet I was not pleased. The place had all the charms it used to have when I was most satisfied with it; and, had you been there, I should have liked it much more than ever I did. But that not being, it was no more to me than the next field."

Temple, it must be admitted found her at times a trifle too restrained—at any rate during the first month of their correspondence. Need she end her letters to him "your humble servant" he asked; and could she not call their sentiment for one another love, instead of friendship? His ardour could not fail to thaw her a little. She stopped saying "your humble servant". The word "love" however, still stuck in her throat. This shrinking was due less to personal disinclination—did he not in fact entirely possess her heart—than to an uncertainty as to the prospects of their marrying, which made her hesitate to let herself go completely. These prospects were, if possible, more uncertain than ever. Dorothy had declared to Temple earlier in their correspondence that her principles forbade her to consider marrying him without her family's consent. As the months passed, the Osbornes began to get wind of her renewed intimacy with Temple, and their opposition increased. Sir Peter himself did not take much part in it, he was too old and too ill. But his place was filled, more than adequately, by her relations. Her two brothers, her aunt Lady Gargrave, cousin Thorold, and cousin Molle were at Dorothy so continuously about it, that she scarcely knew which way to turn. Uneventful as life at Chicksands might seem to the casual observer, it was, throughout the summer of 1653, the scene of an ever-intensifying struggle. It was not an open struggle. Dorothy took care not to enlighten her family fully about her situation, for fear of provoking them to a definite prohibition: while the Osbornes, ignorant precisely how far she was committed to Temple, shrank from assuming too much, for fear of antagonizing her irretrievably. It seems likely that they, like other people, were a little frightened of Dorothy. Accordingly, the campaign was conducted by hints, speaking silences and awkward questions. The Osbornes' proposed suitors talked a great deal of the importance of marrying prudently, and regretted loudly that so agreeable a man as Temple was not eligible. On her side, Dorothy, while making no objection to marriage in theory, found good reasons for refusing each particular match. To their hints about Temple, she presented a front of demure impassivity. Besides resisting the attacks of her family in force, she had to be on her guard against individual onslaughts on her firmness of mind. Lady Gargrave bombarded her with invitations to London in order to meet new suitors; her elder brother would suddenly ask her with a teasing, meaning smile, if she had heard that Temple was going to be married. These last attacks did not worry Dorothy very much. She could always tell Lady Gargrave that Sir Peter was too ill for her to leave Chicksands. And her elder brother—genial easy-going John

Osborne—was, she knew, too like herself in his hatred of a row, ever to push things disagreeably far.

It was very different with her brother Henry. Colonel Henry Osborne was the most formidable of all Temple's opponents. From the fitful glimpses of his figure that flit across the pages of Dorothy's correspondence, and which are all we know of him, he emerges as an extremely difficult character; unbalanced, ungoverned, and egotistic, an uneasy mixture of worldly cunning and uncontrolled impulses of passion. Moreover, his opposition was actuated by a different and more compelling motive than that of her other relatives. He was possessed by a strange and obsessing love for Dorothy—a stranger, she said, would take his letters to her for love letters written to a mistress—which made him violently jealous lest she should care deeply for anyone else. That she would have to marry, he recognized as inevitable; but at all costs let it not be for love. With the sharp eye of jealousy he divined her feeling for Temple: and, since he was a bachelor without a profession, and could, therefore, spend a great deal of time at Chicksands, he put all his energies into the task of preventing its fulfilment. He produced suitor after unattractive suitor, he spied on her during her visits to London, he questioned the servants as to what she did when alone, he searched her drawers for letters, he tried to intercept the post from London. Above all, he argued with her. Sometimes assuming a false air of judicial calm, he urged the paramount importance of wealth and rank in a husband: at others, more ardently, he expatiated on the transience of passion and the disastrous consequences of yielding to it. Then again, he would try by a thousand devices to get her to betray herself about Temple, or he would paint a pathetic picture of his own sufferings, should she ever make a breach between him and her; or, his voice rising in anger, he would threaten to pursue her with unrelenting hostility should she marry without his approval. Dorothy was far from being unmoved by his pleadings. She hated distressing anyone; and, besides, she seems to have felt a deep, though painful, affection for him. However, there was no question of her giving in. Night after night the contest would go on, often with both of them in tears, till the candles were guttering in their sockets and twelve, one, and two o'clock had, in turn, reverberated through the midnight quiet of the house. Feeling had sometimes grown so high that for a time they were hardly on speaking terms. Then Henry, in a revulsion of feeling would apologize, and the quarrel would be made up, only to break out with renewed violence a day or two later. "We have had such a skirmish and on so foolish an occasion", so runs a typical account of one of these scenes. "The Emperor and his proposals began it. I talked merrily on, until I saw my brother put on his sober face; and could hardly then believe he was in earnest. It seems he was; for, when I had spoke my meaning, it wrought so with him as to fetch up all that lay upon his stomach. All the people that I had ever in my life refused were brought again upon the stage, like Richard III's ghosts, to reproach me with. . . . Well, 'twas a pretty lecture and I grew warm with it after a while; and, in short, we came so near an absolute falling out, that it was time to give over; and we said so much then, that we have hardly spoken a word together since. But 'tis wonderful to see what courtesies and legs pass between us; and, as before we were thought the kindest brother and sister, we are certainly now the most complimentary couple in England. 'Tis a strange chance and I am sorry for it; but I will swear I know not how to help it. I look upon it as one of my great misfortunates, and I must bear it, as that which is not my first, nor likely to be my last."

Henry Osborne became so obsessed about Dorothy and Temple, that, besides tormenting her about the subject, he held forth on it to everyone he met; with the result that it became the talk of the county. This was peculiarly upsetting to

Dorothy, with her horror of publicity. Altogether the situation was a great and growing strain on her nerves; a strain which began to betray itself in her letters. Temple remarked it. Early in the summer, in order to ease the tension, he wrote offering to release her from any formal engagement. When everything was so uncertain, would she not be happier if she felt herself absolutely free? Such a thought had never entered Dorothy's head. "Alas," she cried, "alas, if I could purchase the Empire of the world at that rate, I should think it much too dear!" His chivalry in making such a proposal bound her all the closer to him. But it could not remove the causes of her uneasiness; and, do what she would, the tone of her letters continued gloomy. She could promise him confidently not to marry anyone else—except under duress—but, she said, had not they better face the fact that the prospects of their being able to marry each other were almost nil. Temple exclaimed against such pessimism. She replied to his exclamations with the tartness of a spirit thoroughly on edge. "You must pardon me if I cannot agree to give you false hopes," she said. "I must be deceived myself before I can deceive you; and I have so accustomed myself to tell you what I think, that I must either say nothing or that which I believe to be true." Such a retort was not of a kind to tranquillize Temple. The situation was beginning to tell on his nerves too. His active masculine spirit chafed at delay. If Dorothy did not want to break the engagement off, why was he not able to marry her at once? Moreover, as we have seen, indefinite frustration had a peculiarly exacerbating effect on his highly-geared nervous organization. His feelings of exasperation began to break out in sudden impulses of irritation and suspicion. He accused Dorothy of being severe, unjust, unmerciful, unkind; she wrote too seldom or too shortly; once more he would harp on her lack of demonstrativeness; he was seized with a jealous fear lest her suitors might in the end prevail. After all, they were on the spot and he was not. Could he not come down to Chicksands, he asked? No, said Dorothy, Henry might be there, and would think that she had asked Temple in order to annoy him. If, on the other hand, he came when Henry was away, she would appear to be acting in an underhand fashion. For fear of this she even refused to suggest going to Epsom Wells for her health again, lest Henry should suspect she went in order to meet Temple. It was so much against Dorothy's most sacred and traditional instincts to oppose the lawful authority of her family, that she could only bring herself to do so as long as she was absolutely sure that she was taking no action that might give them a legitimate grievance against her. All she could do was to tell Temple again and again, how much she longed to see him; and, for the time being, to try and soothe him, now by gently laughing at his violence, now by earnestly protesting her love. Her own mood was too anxious for her to be able to do either with the right kind of conviction. There was little heart in her jokes; and her protestations were backed by no confident hope in the future.

Prospects were no brighter during the months that followed. In one respect Dorothy might have been expected to feel easier. What with her own obduracy and the rumours about Temple, her suitors one by one had begun to drop away. By the autumn almost all were married, even Sir Justinian. "The spiteful man, merely to vex me, has gone and married", commented Dorothy. "What a multitude of willow-garlands shall I wear before I die! I think I had best to make some into faggots this cold weather; the flame they would make in the chimney would be of more use to me than that which was in the hearts of all those that gave them me, and would last as long." This defection of her lovers, however, so far from tranquillizing Dorothy's situation only intensified her family's anxiety that she should marry soon, before all her chances were gone. New suitors were produced, new arguments put forward; Henry Osborne showed himself as temperamental as ever.

Certainly country life at Chicksands that autumn was not cheerful. In September the atmosphere was further darkened by the news that Dorothy's brother Robin had suddenly died. Dorothy herself was less distressed by this than one might have expected, considering how fond she was of her family. She hardly mentioned her loss to Temple except to say what a good thing it was that so few people saw her nowadays—she looked such a fright in mourning—and was surprised that her oldest brother should not be in better spirits seeing that he had inherited Robin's fortune. The truth was that her love for Temple now filled her heart so completely as to render all other ties unimportant to her. "Sure", she says, "I am not insensible only from ill-nature; and yet I will swear I think I do not afflict myself half so much as another would do, that had my losses. I pay nothing of sadness to the memory of my poor brother, but I presently disperse it with thinking what I owe in thankfulness that 'tis not you I mourn for." Still, Robin Osborne's death added to her general feeling of melancholy. Once more she wondered if, born to misfortune, she was fated to lose everyone dear to her.

Temple's letters did nothing to reassure her. Now that his sense of frustration had been roused, it had made its usual violent effect on his moody temperament. Dorothy was horrified to hear how changed he appeared. No longer sanguine and social, he spent his days alone and plunged in depression. At the same time, inconsistently, he scolded her for what he considered the shocking pessimism of her outlook. How mistaken too it was of her to suggest that unhappiness might be good for the character! More insistently than ever he besought her to come to London. Once Dorothy explained that this was her first wish, but at the moment it was impossible for her to find anyone to take her. Temple does not seem to have been convinced. At any rate, he only increased his urgings. Gradually his unresponsiveness began to react on Dorothy. Her letters still strove to pursue the old tone. She laughed, she coaxed, she sent him her portrait by Lely, she gossiped about Lady Carlyle, but, beneath the polished surface, we can detect a steadily dwindling confidence, an ever-sharpening sense of tension.

At last, towards the end of October, she did contrive to get to London. This second visit, however, though it lasted a month, did not succeed in dissipating the cloud that overhung her spirit. Circumstances were more disagreeable for one thing. Henry Osborne came too, and Dorothy still had to sit up till two in the morning disputing with him. Nor were her interviews with Temple much more peaceful. The friction implicit in their recent letters now showed itself openly. Temple's pent up feelings burst out in passionate pleading. If Dorothy persisted in pointing out the difficulties of the position, he turned on her with accusations of inconstancy and hard-heartedness. She parted from him only to lie awake in anguish; and then, when dawn broke, to rush to her writing-table to scribble a note of explanation and apology.

"I have slept as little as you and may be allowed to talk as unreasonably. Yet I find I am not quite senseless; I have a heart still that cannot resolve to refuse you anything within its power to grant . . . I do but ask though, do what you please, only believe you do a great injustice if you think me false. I never resolve to give you a final farewell, but I resolve at the same time to part with all the comfort of my life; and, whether I told you or not, I shall die

Yours,
Dorothy.

Tell me what you will have me do."

No—the longed-for, waited-for, hardly-achieved meeting had proved no solution of her difficulties. And, when back at Chicksands, alone but for the old knight dying upstairs, and amid the echoing faded walls of the great house, standing solitary in the damp, low-lying countryside under the sad November sky, she began to review her situation, a perturbation such as she had not known before, began to invade her spirit. People who had not seen her since she went to London thought she must have been very ill there; she looked so ghastly. Well she might! She had come to the crisis of her history. Two impulses dominated in Dorothy. She was a born lover, one of those natures which can only find its fulfilment in the art and ecstasy of love. But almost equally strong in her was that fundamental distrust of life implanted in her by the misfortunes of her early years. These two impulses were not compatible. To satisfy her gift for love, she must accept experience with all the risks attendant on it. Her distrust of life, on the other hand, inclined her to shrink from experience as bound to bring her to disaster. From the time she had first met Temple, the two had been at war within her heart. It was a hard struggle for her distrust had powerful allies—absence, uncertainty, family influence, regard for established authority and, simply, the loss of heart induced by long delay. All the same, for eight years her love had proved strong enough to keep the ascendant. But now a new force arose to enlist itself in the armies of opposition. The irritation produced by the strain of the situation had begun to make itself felt in the relation between her and Temple, with the result that her very tenderness for him began to sap the force of her resistance. If her engagement was to involve quarrelling not only with her relations, but with Temple himself, then Dorothy—exhausted with four years' struggle—felt she could hardly bring herself to face the ordeal of going on with it. Perhaps she had better give him up. After all, her instinct had always told her that passion was a dangerous thing. And her creed too: her fear of life now began to rationalize itself as a conviction that her love was, in itself, sinful. Was it not idolatry to offer to a mortal that adoration which was due to God alone? A superstitious sense of guilt began to obsess her. She felt that God had raised up so many obstacles against her reunion with Temple because he disapproved of it; that her sufferings were a punishment rightly inflicted on her for loving man more than God; and that now as a final penalty, love itself was to be poisoned. What then ought to be done? How was God's wrath to be allayed. There was only one way surely, the way of sacrifice. If the lovers voluntarily were to give each other up, then punishment for sin might be averted, and peace descend upon the soul once more.

Thus, during the long lonely hours with autumn darkening to winter round her, Dorothy endlessly and tormentedly brooded. Thus steadily the force of her love gave ground to the forces of her fear. At last, in December, she hesitated no longer; and sitting down, in as controlled a tone as she could command, she wrote to Temple breaking it off.

"I have seriously considered all our misfortunes, and can see no end to them but by submitting to that which we cannot avoid, and, by yielding to it, break the force of a blow which, if resisted, brings a certain ruin. I think I need not tell you how dear you have been to me, nor that in your kindness I placed all the satisfaction of my life; 'twas the only happiness I proposed to myself, and had set my heart so much upon it that it was therefore made my punishment, to let me see that, how innocent soever I thought my affection, it was guilty in being greater than is allowable for things of this world. 'Tis not a melancholy humour gives me these apprehensions and inclinations, nor the persuasions of others; 'tis the result of a long strife with myself, before my reason could overcome my passion, or bring me to a perfect resignation to whatever is allotted for me. . . .

We have lived hitherto upon hopes so airy that I have often wondered how they could support the weight of our misfortunes; but passion gives a strength above nature, we see it in most people; and not to flatter ourselves, ours is but a refined degree of madness. What can it be, to be lost to all things in the world but the single object that takes up one's fancy, to lose all the quiet and repose of one's life in hunting after it, when there is so little likelihood of ever gaining it, and so many more probable accidents that will infallibly make us miss on't. And which is more than all, 'tis being mastered by that which reason and religion teaches us to govern, and in that only gives us a pre-eminence over beasts . . . as we have not differed in anything else, we could agree in this too, and resolve upon a friendship that will be much the perfecter for having nothing of passion in it. How happy might we be without so much as a fear of the change that any accident could bring! We might defy all that fortune could do, and putting off all disguise and constraint, with that which only made it necessary, make our lives as easy to us as the condition of this world will permit. I may own you as a person that I extremely value and esteem, and for whom I have a particular friendship, and you may consider me as one that will always be

Yours faithful
Dorothy Osborne."

Temple was not prepared to consider anything of the kind. In spite of his own offer to release her from the embarrassments of a formal engagement, in spite of his recent fits of despondency, he had not, since their reunion, ever conceived of giving Dorothy up. He answered her letter at once and in a

fury. Far from accepting the view that it was his duty to break
with her, he refused to believe that she thought it their duty
either. All this pious talk of hers was just a hypocritical mask
for weakness, perhaps for ambition. It was likely enough, as
far as he could see, that she was breaking with him in order to
marry Henry Cromwell. For the rest, he announced his intention of coming down to Chicksands immediately, in order
to have it out with her.

Dorothy's first reaction to this onslaught was anger. Temple
thought only of himself; he did not make the slightest effort
to understand her; he positively wanted to make her miserable. For what else could he mean by insisting on coming to
Chicksands. She was not going to change her mind. The only
purpose his visit could serve was to render her situation in the
world even more intolerable than before. Already, as an
earnest of the finality of her decision, she had formally announced to her brother Henry that all was over between her
and Temple. What was he likely to think of her if she now
received on familiar terms a man she did not intend to marry?
Her good name was the only thing of value left her; now
Temple seemed to want to deprive her of that. Anyway, she
simply must insist on his not coming till after Christmas.
Christmas she intended to dedicate to her devotions and for
her devotions she must try and preserve some tranquillity of
spirit. As a symbol of her considered change of heart, she
signed this second letter in the earlier colder form "your
humble servant". Dorothy allowed herself to write all the
more strongly because her genuine anger was reinforced by
her desire to sacrifice herself. To arouse Temple's hostility
was possibly the only way to make him agree to the breach.
If so, it was her duty to make their quarrel as bitter as possible.

Dorothy's conception of her duty seemed to be growing
more and more painful. Indeed, her decision had done nothing
as yet to bring her that peace of soul she longed for. The

agonies of irresolution had left her only to be succeeded by a numb lassitude of despair. Temporarily, her capacity for emotion was exhausted. She wished for nothing, she longed for nothing. Even those relatives she was fondest of no longer stirred in her the slightest feeling of affection. Her heart, she said, with a sad topical irony, was like a country after a civil war, so ravaged as to be of no use to anyone. The truth was that love had grown to be the necessary element of Dorothy's existence. Deprived of it, life in this world was literally not worth living to her; and, in fact, now that she surveyed it in the bleak light of her renunciation, there welled up in her spirit a wave of disgust at the whole miserable ignoble spectacle. How bitterly justified her distrust of the world had proved! Death was preferable to life. There were moments when Dorothy longed for death. "May I enjoy", she said, "an early and a quiet grave, free from the trouble of this busy world, where all with passion pursue their own interests at their neighbours' charges; where nobody is pleased, but somebody complains on't; and where it is impossible to be, without giving and receiving injuries." What must have made Dorothy's desolation worse was that she had to keep it a secret. Christmas was upon her; and she must needs take part in the heavy elaborate junketings with which the seventeenth century thought fit to celebrate that festival, was forced to smile and converse, dine out, and entertain parties at Chicksands, all without betraying a sign of her inner suffering.

However, her ordeal was nearly at its period. Dorothy's obstinacy had not succeeded in persuading Temple to resignation. On the contrary, it had made him realize, as never before, how acute was the danger of losing her; with the result that all the force of his vehement and wilful temperament rose up in frantic resistance. He became so beside himself that Sir John Temple, who was staying in London at the time, did not like to let him out of his sight; he was afraid his son might do himself an injury. And indeed Temple did write a wild letter to Dorothy threatening apparently to kill himself if she persisted.

Thunderstruck with horror Dorothy read his words. Here was a development she had not reckoned with. Her anger, her insensibility, even her deep concern for the honour of her name were instantly forgotten in the flood of terrified tenderness that swept over her at the thought of his condition. Almost distraught at what he must be going through, she dashed off to him first one letter, then another, conjuring him, by any love he had ever felt for her, to moderate the extravagance of his emotion.

"Sir, if you ever loved me do not refuse the last request I shall ever make; 'tis to preserve yourself from the violence of your passion. Vent it all upon me; call me and think me what you please; make me, if it be possible, more wretched than I am. I will bear it all without the least murmur. Nay, I deserve it all. And had you never seen me you would certainly be happy. 'Tis my misfortunes that have this infectious quality as to strike me, and all that is dear to me . . . . If I ever forget what I owe you or ever entertain a thought of kindness for any person in the world besides, may I live a long and miserable life. 'Tis the greatest curse I can invent: if there be a greater may I feel it. This is all I can say. Tell me if it be possible I can do anything for you, and tell me how I may deserve your pardon for all the trouble I have given you. I would not die without it."

And again, an hour or two later:

"If I loved you less I would allow you to be the same person to me, and I would be the same to you as heretofore. But to deal freely with you, that were to betray myself, and I find that my passion would quickly be my master again if I gave it any liberty. I am not secure that it would not make me do the most extravagant things in the world, and I shall be forced to keep a continual war alive with it as long as there are any remainders of it left;—I think I might as well have said as long as I lived. Why should you give yourself over so unreasonably to it? Good God! no woman breathing can deserve half the trouble you give yourself. If I were yours from this minute I could not recompense what you have suffered from the violence of your passion, though I were all that you can imagine me, when, God knows, I am an inconsiderable person, born to a thousand misfortunes, which have taken away all sense of anything else from me, and left me a walking misery only. I do from my soul forgive you all the injuries your passion has done me, though, let me tell you, I was much more at my ease whilst I was angry. Scorn and despite would have cured me in some reasonable time, which I despair of now. However, I am not displeased with it, and if it may be of any advantage to you, I shall not consider myself in it; but let me beg, then, that you will leave off these dismal thoughts. I tremble at the desperate things you say in your letter; for the love of God, consider seriously with yourself what can enter into comparison with the safety of your soul. Are a thousand women, or ten thousand worlds, worth it? No, you cannot have so little reason left as you pretend, nor so little religion. For God's sake let us not neglect what can only make us happy, for trifles."

Dorothy may reiterate her religious scruples. But the pleading uncertain tone of these last letters is very different from that of her former communications. Temple noticed it at once: he also noticed that in the tumult of her anxiety, she admitted the ardour of her love more freely than ever before. He redoubled his efforts to persuade her to weaken. Dorothy's resolution had been the result of too long and too painful a process for her to yield at once. But, in fact, the tide of her feeling had turned. For that factor, which had just swayed the scale in her original decision, had now lost its force. She had managed to screw herself up to breaking with Temple only because she thought that the engagement was making him miserable; and that, in the end, he might be happier if he were free. Now she saw that the only result of her action had been to render him more unhappy than before. She found that she was driving the man whose happiness was the object of her every thought and feeling, into frenzied despair. This was more than she could face. It was not that she felt any more hopeful about the future. Her reason still told her there was little chance their engagement would end in marriage; but no longer did she feel that she could herself take the responsibility of putting an end to it. For a week she hesitated. Then she wrote giving in completely. Since Temple's love seemed to be incurable, she might as well own to him that hers was too. Of course she would marry him, even if it meant waiting indefinitely. Only they simply must try not to make the strain worse than it need be, by quarrelling with each other: no more doubts, no more jealousies.

The most dangerous crisis in their relationship had passed: and a major crisis in Dorothy's inner life. Renunciation would have meant her spiritual ruin. For love was her vocation: her distrust of life, whether justified or not by the facts of human history, was a negative force, an alien destructive importation that could only thwart the fruitful fulfilment of her nature. That it was defeated was due to Temple: and ironically enough, to his faults as much as to his virtues. His sanguine fire, it is true, had, as always, revived her fainting spirit. But his egotism had helped too. He had simply refused to enter into

her feelings in so far as they were opposed to his desires; so that her instinct for self-sacrifice, perverted temporarily to support the dictates of her fear, was now forcibly recalled to the service of her love. If Temple would not look at things from ʰer point of view, she had no choice but to look at them from his. Luckily, on this occasion his happened to be the right one. Selfishness is sometimes necessary to salvation.

Their reconciliation was sealed by a meeting. Temple paid a flying visit to Chicksands. It was a little awkward, for Henry Osborne was still there, and Dorothy did not dare tell him that the engagement was on again. However, she got out of the difficulty by explaining, truthfully as it happened, that Temple was about to go and stay with his father, who had just left London to settle in Ireland, and that he had only come to say goodbye. Fortunately, when the time came for Temple to depart, the lovers appeared so depressed that Henry thought they must be taking a final farewell of one another. Indeed, during their brief snatched tantalizing time together, the excitement of seeing Temple and reaction after the blank despair of the previous weeks, did combine to throw Dorothy into a strange turmoil of conflicting emotions—gaiety and sadness, anxiety and relief. The day sped by in a dazed dream; after Temple had gone, she remembered a hundred things she had meant to say to him, and forgotten in her confusion of mind. However, she had said the only things that mattered. In the sunlight of each other's presence, the last thin shadow of misunderstanding had vanished. They parted more closely bound to one another than ever before. A week or two later, as a pledge of their bond, Temple sent her a ring—gold, with a tortoishell guard. Inside it was engraved a couplet expressive of their sworn and secret faith—

"The love I owe
I cannot showe."

They also exchanged locks of hair. Alone in her room for hours together Dorothy would gaze at Temple's curling handsome tress, and kiss it, and comb it, and go to bed to dream of it, in a trance of happy love.

Meanwhile, to outward appearance, the course of her life had slipped back into its old grooves. Her letters, save that they are suffused ever so delicately with a brighter glow of sentiment, are written in the same tone and about the same topics as those of the previous summer. Once more the picture of those quiet days recomposes itself for us. Now Dorothy is wandering into the garden in her nightgown very early on a fine morning, now whiling away an evening drawing Valentines with Jane Wright, now asking Temple to get her some tweezers, now gossiping. "What did Temple think of Lady Ruthven marrying a man who clacked like a mill?" she asked; "what a number of marriages seemed to be breaking up! How surprisingly loose the manners of young people had grown!" Dorothy put this last phenomenon down to the absence of a Court. There was no longer any accepted social authority, she said, to set a standard, and maintain convention; and few people were strong enough morally not to be better for submitting their wills to authority. This last reflection struck Temple as savouring dangerously of her old defeatist habit of mind. He protested. Dorothy replied teasingly that she found support for her view in the works of no less a person that Bishop Jeremy Taylor. She read as much as ever—she would rather read than talk, she said, unless it was to Temple—Taylor's *Holy Living*, Don Fernando Pinto's *Travels in China*, the romance of Parthenissa. And as much as ever she complained about her suitors. For they had begun again. Her elder brother proposed another well-to-do widower for her; and there was a pushing little neighbour called Beverley, who so persecuted her with his attentions that at last, in order to make her feelings quite clear to him, she threw his letters unopened into the fire before his very eyes. Temple remembered Beverley at College; he called him "the whelp". On his side, Beverley thought Temple "the proudest, imperious, insulting, ill-natured man that ever was". It was the impression that Temple usually produced on inferior persons.

Beverley's was not the only abuse of her lover to which Dorothy was forced to listen. Henry Osborne had begun to suspect the engagement was not so much at an end as he had been led to believe. And one night he began violently attacking Temple on the ground that he was a man of no honour and no religion. This last was to Dorothy the most unforgivable accusation that could be brought against anyone. She flared up once more:

"I forgot all my disguise, and we talked ourselves weary; he renounced me and I defied him, but both in as civil language as it would permit and parted with great anger with the usual ceremony of a leg and a courtesy, that you would have died with laughing to have seen us.

The next day I, not being at dinner, saw him not till night; then he came into my chamber, where I supped but he did not. Afterwards Mr. Gibson and he and I talked of indifferent things till all but we two went to bed. Then he sat half an hour and said not one word, nor I to him. At last, in a pitiful tone, 'Sister', says he, 'I have heard you say that when anything troubles you, of all things you apprehend going to bed, because there it increases upon you, and you lie at the mercy of all your sad thought, which the silence and darkness of the night adds a horror to; I am at that pass now. I vow to God I would not endure another night like the last to gain a crown.' I, who resolved to take no notice what ailed him, said 'twas a knowledge I had raised from my spleen only, and so fell into a discourse of melancholy and the causes, and from that (I know not how) into religion; and we talked so long of it, and so devoutly, that it laid all our anger. We grew to a calm and peace with all the world. Two hermits conversing in a cell they equally inhabit, ner'er expressed more humble, charitable kindness, one towards another, than we. He asked my pardon and I his, and he has promised me never to speak of it to me whilst he lives, but leave the event to God Almighty."

When he was in this softened, pathetic mood, Dorothy still found it painful to resist Henry. Indeed, settling down to her old life did entail, in some degree, settling down to her old worries. The practical obstacle confronting the lovers remained. What prospect was there that the Osbornes would ever be brought to approve the marriage? Or Sir John Temple either. For he too was still hostile: he told Temple Dorothy was not worthy of him, that she was behaving very badly, shilly-shallying like this; he made no offer to increase his allowance to Temple. And Temple's lack of money was, officially at any rate, the main obstacle to him in the Osbornes' eyes. Temple, encouraged by his recent victory over her religious scruples, urged Dorothy to pay no attention to this, and marry him all the same. Here, however, she was adamant. It was not only that it was against her principles to disobey her parents. She was also possessed by an extraordinary horror of the scorn and disapproval she would expose herself to from the world at large, if she made what it would consider an imprudent marriage. Again and again, with hysterical emphasis she refers to this feeling.

"Possibly it is a weakness in me to aim at the world's esteem, as if I could not be happy without it. But there are certainly things that custom has made almost of absolute necessity; and reputation I take to be one of those. If one could be invisible, I should choose that; but since all people are seen and known and shall be talked of in spite of their teeth, who is it that does not desire at least that nothing of ill may be said of them whether justly or otherwise? I never knew any so satisfied with their own innocence as to be content the world should think them guilty. Some out of pride have seemed to condemn ill-reports, when they have found they could not avoid them; but none out of strength of reason, though many have pretended to it."

This nervous regard for public opinion is at first glance extremely mysterious to a modern reader. It seems inconsistent alike with Dorothy's passion, her unworldliness and her independence of mind. Was it vanity? Temple suggested so, in a spasm of irritation. But, replied Dorothy truthfully, no one ever cared less for admiration than she did; her most cherished wish was to pass through life unnoticed. Nor was she conventional in the sense that she accepted standards without question just because they were held by the majority. Yet it is true that the ideas of her rank and her period do partly account for her attitude. To the Caroline gentry public reputation was inextricably bound up with private honour: it was part of a man's duty to himself not to drag his good name in the mud. And, since the order of society was thought to have a divine sanction, the Carolines thought it a very serious act to incur the considered disapproval of its most respect-worthy members. Nor was there any doubt that to marry imprudently did mean incurring such disapproval. Marriage to them, as to the French still, was not the culmination of a love affair, but an essential part of the social system, whose function it was to maintain the institution of the family. As such it must rest on a sound financial basis. To marry in disregard of this, and from purely sentimental reasons, was a feckless act which no conscientious person would have felt justified in committing. Dorothy was far too conscientious not to agree with this view.

She embraced it so desperately, however, from deeper and less rational motives. Dorothy could feel neither the confidence in her own judgment to challenge public opinion, nor the strength of spirit to endure its disapproval. Her bruised nerves flinched uncontrollably at the prospect of publicity and obloquy and misunderstanding. Better to avoid them by conforming to established custom. Even if she suffered all the same, it would be custom's responsibility, not her's; and as such easier to bear. Moreover, to engage in a fight one must, like Temple, be encouraged by the faith one will win. In her darker moods Dorothy was without such a faith. Do what she would, she could not rid herself of the feeling that she was peculiarly doomed to disappointment. It was the old trouble. Deep psychological wounds are not so easily healed. After the first exhilaration of her reconciliation with Temple had worn off, Dorothy's morbid distrust of life raised its head once more. Her deference to convention, like her sense of sin, was only an attempt to find some rational justification for it. And though she strove to argue the case for prudence in cool and reasonable tones, after a paragraph or two she falters, to let the inexplicable foreboding that haunted her heart tremble forth in a sigh of hopeless yearning.

"Dear, shall we ever be so happy, think you? Ah I dare not hope it; yet 'tis not want of love that gives me these fears. No, in earnest I think—nay I am sure—I love you more than ever, and 'tis that only gives me these despairing thoughts. When I consider how small a proportion of happiness is allowed in this world, and how great mine would be in a person for whom I have a passionate kindness, and who has the same for me; as it is infinitely above what I can deserve and more than God Almighty usually allots to the best people, I can find nothing in reason but seems to be against me; and methinks 'tis as vain in me to expect it, as t'would be to hope I might be a Queen."

"Shall we ever be so happy?"—it is not the first time she has said it. The wistful little phrase echoes like a refrain through all her correspondence.

Nevertheless, in spite of occasional fits of melancholy, Dorothy was in better spirits than ever before. The fact that the forces of her distrust had been defeated in the decisive battle of December had permanently weakened their hold over her. There was no more any question, even when she was feeling most despondent, of her voluntarily giving up Temple. Her confidence was gradually growing. By the beginning of March it was strong enough to make her, for the first time, take the offensive in her conflict with her family. She announced to Henry that she was engaged to Temple. Two days later fate, whom she had so long and so justifiably counted her enemy, came to her aid. Sir Peter Osborne died. In the first shock of bereavement a wave of depression swept over Dorothy. Not only had she loved him with peculiar tenderness—he had been peculiarly affectionate to her—but she felt very lonely. Her home was taken from her; and, since in those days it was not thought possible for a young lady to set up house on her own, Dorothy, shy, proud and twenty-six years old, was faced with the prospect of making her life as a dependant in the home of whatever member of her family would have her. Considering how strained her relations with them had lately been, she did not expect to find them sympathetic companions. "Kindred, not friends," she called them; and she complained to Temple that, though she was to pay them as much for her keep as though she were a stranger, they still thought they were doing her a kindness. All the same, as regards the crucial issue of her life, she was better off. Brothers and aunts had not the legal authority over her that a parent had; and she did not feel the same moral obligation to respect their wishes. It was much easier for her to marry whom she liked. All the more so that Henry in particular now began to put himself even more in the wrong than before. Utterly insensitive to any sorrow she might be feeling, he began arguing with her about Temple within twenty-four hours of her father's death; and, when he found her firm, relieved his feelings by lamenting to all and sundry that his sister had gone and engaged herself to an arrogant and impecunious atheist. Dorothy's fighting spirit rose. She had tied up her hands, she told Henry, so that she could not marry anyone but Temple. Moreover, if everyone was to know about her engagement, let them know it officially. No longer did she wish to keep it a secret. This was a great step forward. With Dorothy committed in the eyes of the world, it was much harder for the Osbornes to make her withdraw. Anyway, in the tenacious mood she now showed herself, they began to despair of ever making her give way. Things were growing easier on the Temple side too. Under the continual and tempestuous pressure of his son, Sir John had begun to waver in his opposition, and, apparently, offered to give him some more money. In face of this the Osbornes could resist no longer. Even Henry resigned himself, and for the time being spoke kindly to Dorothy about it. By the beginning of the summer both sides had, in principle at any rate, agreed to the match.

All anxiety was not over though. Getting married in those circles was like making an international treaty. Indeed it was a sort of treaty—a financial treaty, in which preliminaries must be laid down, representatives appointed, negotiations conducted according to carefully prescribed forms, before the final settlement was arrived at. And at each step a fatal hitch might occur. Throughout the summer months the stately interminable business proceeded, impeded at every turn by objections and qualifications: and, until the last document was signed, no one could be quite sure that the marriage would come off. Certainly, Dorothy could not be. Do what she would Dorothy could not acquire the habit of hope: and the hint of a set-back sent a chill of discouragement coursing through her. Luckily however, her love had now established a permanent ascendancy over her despondency. Against her strongest instincts, and simply because she knew Temple wanted her to, she did her best to combat despair. "I hope merely because you bid me" she said sadly, "and lose that hope as often as I consider anything but yours. Would I were easy of belief! They say one is so to all that one desires. I do not find it." No amount of good fortune could completely cure Dorothy of her temperamental weakness.

Nor could it cure Temple of his. Early in May, while he was still in Ireland, he did not hear from her for several weeks. It was the fault of the postal service; Temple might have been expected to guess this, after all that had happened. Instead, however, he was at once in a fever of nervous suspicion and anxiety, scarcely allayed when her letter did arrive.

"Well now in very great earnest," he wrote, "do you think 'tis time for me to come or no? Would you be very glad to see me there? And could you do it in less disorder and with less surprise than you did at Chicksands? . . . I know you love me still, you promised it me, and that is all the security I can have for all the good I am ever like to have in this world. 'Tis that which makes all things else seem nothing to it, so high it sets me; and so high indeed that should I ever fall, t'would dash me all to pieces. Methinks your very charity should make you

65

love me more now than ever, by seeing me so much more unhappy than I used, by being so much further from you. . . . Justice I am sure will oblige you to it, since you have no other means left in the world of rewarding such a passion as mine, which, sure, is of a much richer value than anything in the world besides. Should you save my life again, should you make me absolute master of your fortune and your person too, yet, if you love me not, I should accept none of all this in any part of payment, and look upon you as one behind hand with me still. 'Tis not vanity this, but a true sense of how pure and how refined a nature my passion is, which none can ever know besides my own heart, unless you find it out by being there. . . .

How hard it is to think of ending when I am writing to you. But it must be so, and I must ever be subject to other people's occasions and so never, I think, master of my own."

Up to the very altar, Temple was to remain the most agitated and Dorothy the most pessimistic of lovers.

This particular letter of Temple's reached her in London. Since Sir Peter's death her mode of life had undergone a swift and sensational change. After six years seclusion in the shadowed backwater of Chicksands, she found herself swept into the glaring rushing midstream of the world. No longer had she a regular home; for the time being her life passed in a succession of country visits followed by a month or two in London. Even there she changed her lodgings every few weeks, according as it was convenient for her friends to take her in. With none of them did she find a tranquil existence. London social life under the Commonwealth was less sober than might have been expected. The playhouses were, it is true, closed, and at any moment political events might rudely interrupt the course of private existence. Dorothy was stopped going on a visit to the country because a plot had been

discovered against Cromwell's life; and till all the conspirators
had been rounded up, no one was allowed to leave London.
Still, people bred of a life of pleasure generally can contrive to
keep it going in some degree, however unpropitious their
circumstances. The aristocracy dined with each other every
night; such places of public amusement, as were still open, were
crammed; from her window in the Strand, Dorothy watched
the sporting set of the Beau Monde driving off to the races.
She took part in fashionable life, as well as observing it. New
faces, new places crowded in on her. Now she is off to dine
at the Swan Tavern; now going masked with a party to walk
in Spring Gardens: now visiting the celebrated Samuel
Cooper to commission him to paint her miniature; now
having her fortune told by the famous astrologer, Lilly.
Dorothy was not impressed by his powers. "No old woman,
who passes for a witch, could have been more puzzled
what to say to reasonable people than he was. He asked us
more questions than we did him."

Indeed, she was not dazzled by the whirling glitter of the
new world into which she had entered. Now and again it
afforded agreeable material for her satiric sense; she found
it entertaining to meet Lady Tollemache for example.

"'Tis not unpleasant methinks to hear her talk, how at
such a time she was sick and the physicians told her she
would have the small-pox, and showed her where they
were coming out upon her; but she bethought herself that
it was not at all convenient to have them at that time.
Some business she had, that required her going abroad, and
so she resolved she would not be sick; nor was not. Twenty
such stories as this she told us; and then falls into discoveries
of the strength of reason and the power of philosophy till
she confounds herself and all that hear her."

On the whole, however, the chief consequence of Dorothy's

encounter with the great world was to confirm her in the conviction that she was unfitted for it. She was too shy for one thing; do what she would, she could not help blushing when she heard Temple's name mentioned. For another, she was incapable of concealing her true opinions. If she thought a party boring—and she was easily bored—she could not help saying so. This did not tend to make her popular with her companions and, as she admitted apologetically to Temple, she knew herself that it did no good. It was a pity to be thought a spoil-sport and a wet blanket even by people who bored one.

In July she left London to spend the rest of the summer with her brother-in-law, Sir Thomas Peyton, at Knowlton, his house in Kent. This was no improvement on London as far as quiet went. "I can only be allowed time to tell you," she writes shortly after her arrival, "that I am in Kent and in a house so strangely crowded with company that I am weary as a dog already." Indeed, staying at Knowlton does sound a great strain. Lady Peyton was a very sociable woman, and life in her house was a continual party, where guests seldom could get to bed till daylight, where they were compelled to take part in private theatricals—Dorothy found herself cast rather ominously for the rôle of the Lost Lady—and so crammed full that she had sometimes to share her bed with two other ladies, and was forced to write to Temple in a room thronged with chattering people. Nor, for the most part, were they sympathetic people. On one night two Colonels arrived to dinner, both revoltingly drunk, and another time when Dorothy said that she wanted to marry a man who would continue to be in love with her all their lives, the young gallants of the party burst into fits of derisive laughter. In addition to this Sir Thomas Peyton, exhausted perhaps by the continual social effort which his wife's tastes compelled him to make, wrangled with her in public all day long. The only people in the house with whom Dorothy felt easy were a lady, grown misanthropic as the result of a quarrel with her husband, and a gentleman whose heart had been broken early in life by the death of his bride to be. These two at least were quiet. But they were not enough to reconcile Dorothy to life at Knowlton. "I would not live thus a twelve month," she writes to Temple in comic desperation, "to gain all that the King has lost, unless it were to give it him again."

Fortunately there was no question of her staying there a twelvemonth. By August events were hurrying to their conclusion. Temple was back from Ireland, and the negotiations for the marriage settlement were fully under way. Before all was over, Dorothy had still to undergo a few painful moments. Her experience of the summer made her recoil with horror from the thought of a public wedding with all its attendant celebrations. Ah! if she could just steal out secretly and marry Temple and drive off! In September too, Sir John Temple suddenly objected to Henry Osborne appearing as a representative of Dorothy's family in the settlement negotiations: he thought he had been too openly hostile to William to deserve such an honour. At this unexpected hitch so near the end of her troubles, Dorothy's strained nerves snapped. After all, Henry was her brother; and, however difficult he may have been in the past, lately he had been making a creditable effort to behave amiably. Besides, she did not think that Sir John had the right to cast a stone; though she had been too considerate of William's feelings to say so at the time, she had in fact been wounded by Sir John thinking her so unworthy a bride for his son. If he persisted in insulting the Osbornes in this way, she burst out, they had better drop the whole thing. It was only a momentary spasm of exasperation. Never was Dorothy less likely to give up Temple than at this juncture. Sir John gave in about Henry and all was soon smoothed over. As a matter of fact,

Henry's subsequent conduct was not to prove such as would have warranted his sister making any sacrifice for his sake. Not only did he begin quarrelling with her again about the marriage at the very last minute, but it was afterwards discovered that he had persuaded her to sign a paper without reading it—on the ground that it was a pure formality—in which she resigned her right to part of her dowry to Henry himself. By the time she found it out, Dorothy now married to Temple, was in no mood to take Henry's side about anything. Feeling grew so high that the families were nearly involved in a law-suit. It is not surprising that during her subsequent life, Dorothy seems never to have had anything more to do with Henry.

But this is to anticipate. By October, at least all was settled. Dorothy came to London for her wedding. We have two little notes she wrote to Temple there; in them her love ripples out, for the first time unqualified by a shadow of anxiety, and sparkling with a sunshiny gaiety, which, coming as it does from one so long forced by hard experience to believe such a mood unattainable, touches us to the heart. "You are like to have an excellent housewife of me. I am abed still and slept so soundly nothing but your letter could have waked me. You shall hear from me as soon as we have done. Farewell! Can you endure that word? No, out upon it, I will see you anon."

And then it turned out that in fact she had been cheerful too soon. Unkindly fate had still a dart in store for Dorothy. A week before her wedding she fell ill with small-pox. It was so bad an attack that the doctors feared for her life. Oblivious of the risk, Temple stayed with her constantly. By December she was out of danger. But small-pox is a cruel disease: Dorothy rose from her bed with her beauty gone. And though Temple married her the moment she was well enough, yet it is related that he found the change in her appearance too great to leave him wholly insensible. It would be unbearably sad to think that his feelings for her were seriously impaired. Nor need we think it. His love, like hers, was grounded on a securer foundation than the perishing red and white of mortal loveliness; on community of tastes, of views, of jokes, on an affinity of the soul. Further, some letters of Dorothy's written two years later breathe a spirit of glad, easy tenderness that could only spring from a union as perfect as any the lovers could have hoped for during the long years of their frustration. She is in the country with her baby Jack: Temple is away on business:

"Can you tell me when you intend to come home. Would you would; I should take it mighty kindly. Good dear make haste. I am as weary as a dog without you. Poor Jack is all the entertainment I have. He remembers his little duty and grows and thrives every day . . . indeed my heart 'tis the quietest best little boy that ever was borne. I am afraid he'll make me grow fond of him, do what I can. The only way to keep me from it is for you to keep at home, for then I am less with him. Now he is all my entertainment, besides what I find in thinking of my dearest and wishing him with his

Dorothy Temple."

The spectre of Dorothy's fears seems laid at last: the distance in her spirit resolved in a final harmonious chord. As in a fairy-tale, the lovers, after trials and troubles innumerable, have settled down to live happily ever after.

*   *   *   *

But had they? Alas, true stories go on after fairy-tales stop; Dorothy lived for forty years more. They were full years too. Men of Temple's energy and talent are not destined to pass their existence in tranquil obscurity, however much they may fancy they would like to. Half unwillingly he found himself drawn for a large part of his life on to the bustling, brightly lit stage of great affairs; where, amid the respectful applause of his contemporaries, he moved through embassies and council chambers and gatherings dedicated to Science and Letters, to end his days, wiser than in his youth, but perhaps a trifle too consciously admirable, living in illustrious retirement amid the apricots and parterres of his delightful house at Moor Park, the trusted counsellor of princes, the stately patron of the youthful Swift. Dorothy supported him in his labours and shared his honours. The records of the day praise her as wife, as ambassadress, as patroness. "Mild Dorothea, peaceful, wise and great"—so Swift extols her. Yet what did she really think of it all? We can only guess; there are no letters left to tell us. But certainly it was a very different sort of existence to that of which she had dreamed in the old days at Chicksands; and there was little time in it for that private life of intimacy and contemplation, in which her heart had laid up its treasure. Moreover, such private life as the Temples did manage to snatch from the pressure of public business, was darkened by catastrophe. Of the six children Dorothy bore to Temple, only one lived to grow up; and he—the little Jack of whom she speaks so lovingly in her last letters—drowned himself in a fit of madness when he was twenty-one. On the occasion of his death we are permitted, after forty years silence, once more to hear Dorothy's voice. She is answering a letter of condolence from a nephew:

"Dear Nephew—I give you many thanks for your kind letter and the sense you have of my affliction, which truly is very great. But since it is laid upon me by the hand of an Almighty and Gracious God, that always proportions His punishments to the support He gives with them, I may hope to bear it as a Christian ought to do, and more especially one that is conscious to herself of having many ways deserved it. The strange revolutions we have seen might well have taught me what this world is, yet it seems it was necessary that I should have a near example of the uncertainty of all human blessings, that so having no tie to the world, I may the better prepare myself to leave it; and that this correction may suffice to teach me my duty must be the prayer of your affectionate aunt and humble servant,

D. Temple."

These are the last words she speaks to us. They make a sad, ironical epilogue to her love-story. For here, though expressed with an austere impersonal formality of phrase strangely unlike the Dorothy of earlier days, is the old sense of guilt, the old disillusioned despondency. Fraught with more tragic overtones, her ancient cry echoes again through our memory. "Shall we ever be so happy?" After all, and in spite of love requited and fulfilled, she had been right to doubt it.

Part Two

THOMAS GRAY

"Voluntary solitude is that which is familiar with melancholy; and gently brings on, like a siren or shoeing-horn or some sphinx, to that irrevocable gulf."

ROBERT BURTON.

THOMAS GRAY

I

THERE is no doubt England's ancient seats of learning present an extremely poetical spectacle. The belfrys of Oxford, the pinnacled vistas of Cambridge, the groves and pensive cloisters of Eton and Winchester, made spiritual by the veil of dewy mist that lingers perpetually over the damp river valleys in which their pious founders have seen fit to place them, induce irresistibly in the visitor a mood of exalted, romantic reverie. It might be thought that their regular inhabitants, exposed at every hour of the day to these dreamy influences, would be among the most poetically-minded of mankind. In fact, however, this is not so. Academic persons are often intellectual and sometimes witty: but seldom indeed are they conspicuous for the poetic qualities, for imagination or aesthetic sensibility. Their very intellectuality has something to do with this. Minds accustomed to concentrate habitually on abstractions tend not to notice their physical environment. On the other hand, however much they may admire academic buildings, people with an artistic temperament seldom take to the academic mode of life. They feel it too bloodless, too conventional, too sheltered from the direct violence of experience to satisfy the passionate intensity of their natures; and fly to uglier but more stimulating surroundings. However, there are exceptions. Now and again an artist is born with enough of the academic in him to make it possible for him to settle in school or college. The diverse strains in him blend to produce a personality of curious and complex fascination to the student of human nature. Walter Pater was such a personality; A. E. Housman was another. But the most elegant example of the type is Gray.

He is also the hardest to understand. This is not for want of information about him. Things had changed since Dorothy Osborne's time. In the fifty odd years that had elapsed between her death and Gray's maturity, England had settled down to an epoch of prosperous stability in which, undisturbed alike by bloodshed or by spiritual yearnings, those, who liked, had been able to concentrate on the development of the private life and the cultivation of its modes of expression. Through the course of their long leisurely lifetimes, some people did little else but talk, write letters, pay visits, and keep journals. They learnt to do it with a fullness and elaborate perfection unsurpassed in history. The private papers of Gray and his friends compose a small library in themselves. All are accomplished, and some—Gray's own letters and those written to him by Horace Walpole—are glittering masterpieces in the art of social intercourse; easy as a casual conversation with an old friend, but made exquisite by every grace of style, every refinement of wit and civility.

All the same, they do not completely reveal their authors. We listen, charmed, to the well-bred voices flowing on in never-ending delightful discourse, now serious, now sparkling, glancing from gossip to antiquities, from literature to the political news; but never stiff, never at a loss, never boring. And then, when we shut the book, it strikes us that there is a great deal about these people we have not been allowed to know. They are acquaintances rather than friends. This reserve is outstandingly characteristic of Gray's circle. The very conscious perfection of their agreeability is partly responsible for it. To them, social intercourse was an art whose aim was to give pleasure. They, therefore, kept it clear of anything they thought unlikely to please. Among

78

these things were personal revelations. They did not even think them interesting. Walpole says openly he disliked letters without news but full of "sentiment". Gray, to judge by his correspondence, shared this opinion. For all their refinement, they, like other people in the eighteenth century, took an extroverted common sense view of life. Objective topics—politics, books, works of art—seemed to them far better worth talking about than the fluctuations of the individual mood, the condition of the individual soul. It was not that they were ashamed of expressing emotion, like a modern public-school boy. If they felt unhappy or affectionate or out of temper, they said so and as eloquently as they could. But they were not interested to analyse these feelings; and they expressed them with a formality of phrase that somehow makes them unintimate.

For—and this is the final cause of their reserve—they believed deeply in form. The spontaneous, the unbuttoned, had no charms for them. They had never doubted that it was a purpose of civilization to impose discipline and polish on the crude natural man. As they wore powdered wigs to cover their naked heads of hair, so they put on a cover of good manners over their naked thoughts and feelings. Their manners were not so ceremonious as those of Dorothy Osborne's day: their tone of voice was more colloquial, their ideal of form less stately. But it affected them more profoundly. For their whole being was saturated with it, it modified their every impulse of thought and feeling. Civilization had moved on since the seventeenth century; and, for Gray and his friends at any rate, it had succeeded in expelling every trace of that naïveté which mingled so strangely with the dignity of Dorothy Osborne's world. Their reactions come to us carefully filtered through the fine firm mesh woven by their standards of good sense and good taste.

No wonder Gray is mysterious to us. Yet he is not unfathomable. Now and again, the man himself breaks through the web: and his personality is present by implication in the ordinary run of his discourse. If we learn to read between the lines, to interpret hint, emphasis, omission, even to guess a little—always remembering that we are guessing—gradually his character and the course of his life begin to take shape before us.

II

From the first we see him in an academic setting. Gray makes his entry on the stage of recorded history as an Eton boy. Not a typical Eton boy, especially of that period. England in the eighteenth century was a robust, red-blooded, uproarious place. The England of Fielding and Hogarth and Parson Woodforde—certainly there was no lack of earthiness there. How people ate and drank! Mountains of beef—hogsheads of port or beer, as the case may be. With what unflagging virile relish they swore, and begat bastards, and gambled and attended executions and proclaimed their belief in liberty and their contempt for the wretched frog-eaters on the other side of the Channel! Eton reproduced in miniature the characteristics of the nation. To a generation bred in the disciplined totalitarianism of the reformed public school, accounts of life there have their charm. There were only four hours of lessons and no compulsory games. There was not much order either; sometimes none. Once or twice in the century open rebellion broke out on a formidable scale. Then authority violently asserted itself, flogging and expelling right and left. But within a short time Eton had relapsed into its customary condition of easy-going anarchy. It was true that if a boy wrote a bad copy of Latin verses, he was summarily and severely birched. But since classes often numbered 100 boys, discipline in school cannot have been very strict.

Out of school they went to bed any hour, they ran off to the races, they gave large parties at the Inn at Windsor, they drank themselves sick with brandy and stuffed themselves with pies at the pastrycook's, they pummelled and beat each other unmercifully. They also enjoyed beating the local rustics. The rustics—for this was still the age of aristocratic ascendancy—were glad enough to let themselves be beaten, if the young gentlemen would throw them a couple of guineas after the operation was over. For the rest, amid the green fields beside the shining Thames with the battlements of Windsor Castle rising in the wooded distance, the boys entertained themselves by staging full-dress fights with bare fists, playing a rough amateurish cricket, or with gleaming bodies bared, diving in the willow-shadowed water. Meanwhile the younger boys—they came as young as nine sometimes—bowled hoops, played leap-frog, or, with long hair flying in the breeze and shrill cries echoing through the air, fled to escape the sudden onslaught of some bullying senior.

Bullying, however, was as unorganized as everything else. The boys of eighteenth century Eton enjoyed the advantages as well as the dangers of freedom. No pressure, moral or physical, was exerted to force those of them who did not wish it, to cultivate the team spirit. And about 1730 a quartet of boys in their teens were to be observed there, who followed a course of life sedulously aloof from that of the mob of high-born ragamuffins by whom they were surrounded. They seldom came into the playing fields at all. If they did, they stood and watched their rampaging schoolfellows from a prudent distance. More often they were to be seen roaming singly by the river, book in hand, or sitting together in the library, absorbed in animated conversation. They gave a general impression of thinness, pallor and graceful preciosity. Their names were Horace Walpole, Richard West, Thomas Ashton and Thomas Gray.

Common tastes and a common unlikeness to other boys had brought them together; for their origins were widely different. Walpole sprang from the resplendent centre of that Whig aristocracy which governed the country; was not his father the great Sir Robert Walpole himself, for over fifteen years all-powerful First Minister of England? West was the son of a lawyer, Ashton of a schoolmaster. Gray came from a less intellectual sphere. His father was a scrivener, and his mother, together with her sister, ran a warehouse in Cornhill. His childhood, it seems, had not been a happy one. Apart from anything else, his background did not suit him. With his intellectual brow, fastidious mouth and elegant little figure, Gray did not look like a product of a Cornhill warehouse. Nor did his appearance belie him. It would be untrue to say that the world he was born in left no mark on Gray: there was always to be a prudent, solid, middle-class streak in him. But blended with it was a scholarly intelligence, an aristocratic pride and, above all, an extraordinary feeling for the charm of the exquisite and the ancestral. This was an imaginative, not a worldly feeling. Within Gray's precise little frame quivered the flame of a passionate sensibility to any manifestation of beauty and romance. Such a disposition was not likely to feel at home in the Hogarthian homeliness of eighteenth century commercial London. The circumstances of his family life did nothing to reconcile him to his family environment. His mother, indeed, was amiable and intelligent. But his father, though reported to be musical, was in other respects a most disagreeable character; morose, brutal and capricious. He spent his wife's money in building a house he did not want, only, it appeared, in order to annoy her, and from the time he married was liable, if irritated, to revile her obscenely and to pummel her in a painful and alarming fashion. So alarming, that later she was driven to ask a lawyer if she had grounds for a legal separation. In those days, how-

THOMAS GRAY AS A BOY

By courtesy of the Syndics of the Fitzwilliam Museum, Cambridge
From a portrait by Jonathan Richardson.

ever, the laws of England looked unfavourably on women who rose in open rebellion against their husband's authority; and Mrs. Gray was told that she had better try and put up with her sufferings for fear of losing her income. Nor, poor lady, was her unpleasing spouse her only source of sorrow. Of the twelve children she bore to him only Thomas survived childhood; and he was not at all strong.

Such a childhood could not fail to have its effect on him. The fact that he identified himself with his mother in her quarrel with his father encouraged the development of a delicate feminine strain in his temperament and intensified a natural distaste for rough masculinity; while the insecurity of the home, where he got his first impressions of the world, implanted in him an ineradicable sense of insecurity about human existence in general. Precociously aware, as he was, of the possibilities of disaster, his free response to experience was chilled and checked. Even as a boy Gray was not spontaneous. There was a touch of doubtful melancholy in the gaze he turned on the world. Already shrinking uncontrollably from the hurly-burly of active life, he sought stability, safety, peace.

However he was not so abnormal as to be incapable of enjoying himself; and his fortunes early took a turn that put enjoyment in his way. In 1725, when he was nine years old, his mother's brother, Roger Antrobus, who was a master at Eton, by way of assisting his struggling sister arranged for Thomas to enter the school, himself paying some of the fees. There Gray remained for the next nine years. These years were crucial in his development. They shaped his taste and coloured his imagination for life. School was likely to influence him powerfully in any case, seeing how early he was transplanted there, and from a home like his. Though he loved his mother, he turned his back on the world she lived in as soon as he could. It was not long before his holidays, spent wretchedly in Cornhill or in forlorn visits to relations, had become nothing but a disagreeable, insignificant interruption to the course of a life whose centre was Eton. It, not Cornhill, became his native country. By the time he was in his teens, all that he enjoyed and valued most was bound up with his existence there.

It was not to be expected that he should enter into the male boisterousness which displayed itself so flamboyantly in the life of the average Etonian. But this does not seem to have worried him. The boys, we are told, thought he was delicate and let him alone. Anyway Eton had other and more congenial satisfactions to offer. There was the beauty of the landscape; the lush sweetness of the Thames valley country, its pastoral charm, as yet unspoilt by urbanization, stretching level into the soft distance, shadowed by the full-foliaged trees, watered by slow sky-reflecting streams, their banks muffled in meadowgrass thick with wild flowers. Gray loved flowers. His Uncle Roger, a keen botanist, noticed this and introduced him to the study. It appealed alike to the student and the artist in him. He spent happy hours collecting and cataloguing butterfly-orchis and bog asphodel.

The works of man at Eton are beautiful too; the time-tinted brick-work of the School Yard, the traceried pile of Chapel, grey between the boles of the lime trees. It is an ancient beauty: Gothic chapel, Tudor clock-tower, Caroline pilastered Upper School, the oak benches of Lower School carved with generation after generation of names—every place in Eton is haunted by ghosts of the past. The youthful Gray responded to its imaginative appeal. The sense of history woke in him to mingle inextricably with his aesthetic sense. For ever after he was to be moved most profoundly by the beauty that is enriched by association with the mystery and romance of a vanished age.

Then there were his lessons; Gray did well at these. He was

a clever boy with a turn for refined exact scholarship. Reading Horace and Virgil was to him a pleasant occupation. As he grew older it became something else—a profound and rapturous experience. Virgil, in particular, with his delicate finish of style, his sad civilized nobility of temper, set vibrating a sympathetic chord in the depths of Gray's spirit. The joy inspired by reading such poetry—what could be compared with it? Nor was it a passive joy. Obscure and unrecognized, in answer to Virgil's silver call, something creative began to stir to life within him. Here, little though he might know it, was to be the mould in which his own personality was to find its supreme expression and fulfilment. "What first gave you a taste for poetry?" someone asked him in later life. "Reading Virgil at Eton as a boy of eleven," said Gray.

Equally important, at Eton he made his first friends. He was not one to be satisfied by solitary pleasures. His lively mind craved someone to talk to; his sensitive heart thirsted for someone to love. Unluckily it was not easy to find either. Fastidiousness and nervousness between them had iced him over with a stiff reserve only to be thawed by someone with whom he felt a genuine affinity of spirit. Gray was not a common type; such people were few. Certainly they were not to be met with in his home circle, nor among the ordinary run of his schoolfellows. However, in so huge and so free a community as that of Eton, even the oddest boy can hope to find a kindred spirit somewhere. Gray found two, Horace Walpole and Richard West. The three had a good deal in common with one another, clever, fragile, unboyish boys who bore all the signs of having been brought up exclusively by doting mothers. Here, however, the likeness between them ends. West shrank from the world even more than Gray; so much so that to strangers he appeared only sickly and insignificant. Shy, fanciful and unworldly, he was at his happiest day-dreaming in the fields or reading and writing verses. His talents bloomed earlier than those of his friends, who thought him a youthful genius. He was far from insignificant to them. Round his meagre figure hovered a lyrical charm in which a pervading minor-key melancholy was occasionally lit up by a flicker of whimsical humour. The deeper strains in Gray found their perfect affinity in West. Here was someone who cared for Virgil and musing just in the same way as he did; here was someone who, like him, felt alone in an alien universe. An intense and intimate affection sprang up between the two, which was to last till death. Hand in hand "like the two children in the wood" they would be seen wandering away to roam the countryside together.

Walpole never penetrated Gray's heart as West did. But he made an even more sensational impression on him. It was no wonder. To a boy brought up like Gray, the youthful Horace Walpole must have been a dazzling apparition indeed. The mere setting of his existence dazzled. It is difficult for us to realize what a huge gulf separated the life of aristocrats in the eighteenth century from that of other people. Fabulously rich, politically omnipotent, and with their superb self-assurance untroubled by the slightest doubt as to their right to a position of unique privilege, they seemed, like the olympian deities in the painted Baroque ceilings which adorned their great houses, to recline, jewelled and garlanded on an aureate cloud, floating far above the drab earth where common mortals trudged through their humdrum existence. From as early as he could remember, whether in his family's Arlington Street mansion, or amid the Palladian architecture of the country seats where he was taken on visits, Horace Walpole had lived in a whirl of high fashion and high politics peopled by the bright figures of courtiers, cabinet ministers, and reigning beauties: and of them he knew his father was the ruling centre. At Eton, on one occasion, he found himself bursting into a torrent of tears at the thought of George I's death, largely, so he tells us, because he thought the son of the Prime Minister ought to be especially moved by such an event. Not that his family life was without its problems. Like Gray's, Walpole's parents did not hit it off. But how differently did they conduct themselves! Good sense, good temper and a large income enabled them to go their own ways satisfactorily while preserving appearances to the world. Easy-going, extravagant Lady Walpole pursued a sociable life in London attended by a succession of lovers; Sir Robert, whose taste was for robuster pleasures, spent the intervals of his political activities at his half-finished palace of Houghton in the jovial company of his mistress, Miss Moll Skerret, keeping open house to a crowd of hard riding, hard drinking hangers-on with whom he exchanged doubtful stories and drank bottle after bottle of port wine. Horace stayed with his mother. As the youngest, cleverest and sickliest of her children he was recklessly indulged and petted. Once, when he was ten, he expressed a desire to see the King: a few days later he was taken off to Kensington Palace for a private audience specially arranged for him after dark, lest the news of it might awake the envy of less privileged persons. Haloed by the glory of such a background, he might well have impressed his schoolfellows, even if he had not been personally remarkable. This, however, was far from being the case. Indeed, for his precocity was freakish, this skinny, vivacious child, with the sharp black eyes and tiptoe walk—"Ariel in slit shoes", as he afterwards described himself—was the same brilliant figure as was to decorate London society for the next sixty years. His schoolboy letters were as accomplished and sophisticated as those of his prime. They are also as inscrutable. Walpole is an even more enigmatic character than Gray. Not only was the delicate, gleaming enamel of his high-bred reserve of a yet more impenetrable quality, but the nature beneath it was inherently more puzzling. There is something para-doxical in the very essence of Horace Walpole. Countless writers have discussed him, but at the end all have confessed themselves baffled. At moments, with his gush, his bric-a-brac and his touchiness, one is tempted to dismiss him as an affected petit-maître who happened to be gifted with a talent for letter writing. One would be wrong, however, to yield to the temptation. Beneath his affectations lay a shrewd knowledge of the world and a steely patrician toughness. He bore agonies of gout without a word of complaint and made it a matter of principle never to wear an overcoat or to change his shoes when he got wet. Again, what are we to make of his taste? His own letters, it is true, are exquisite pieces of art. But in them he admits to thinking nothing of Richardson because his tone was middle-class, or of Johnson because his manners were bearish. This was superficial of him. In a sense he was both superficial and conventional. Ultimate problems bored him: he was satisfied to accept the standards, social and moral, of the world into which he had been born. Yet his superficiality was too deliberate to be completely genuine. Because he preferred it, he chose to remain on life's surface, beautifully polishing it. As for conventions, they never prevented him doing anything he really felt inclined to. If he wanted to decorate his drawing-room like a Gothic Chapel, he did so regardless of what anyone might think.

Even his health was paradoxical. Ailing and feeble from birth, there yet throbbed within him a quenchless vitality that made him able at seventy to dance a quadrille with the zest of an eighteen-year-old. Had he, finally, a heart? Certainly he loved his friends with a fiery affection full of ardours and jealousies, and generous impulses of sympathy. How then was he a born celibate, hating ties, and who, when poor blind old Mme. du Deffand declared her love for him with a frankness which he feared might make him look ridiculous, checked her with a cold ruthlessness that makes one wonder for a moment if he was human at all. Ariel—the name suits more than his appearance; only it is the modish Ariel of the *Rape of the Lock*, not Shakespeare's wild wind-elf. Ageless, sexless, tireless, with his diamond glitter, his waspish irritations, his airy dragon-fly elegance, Horace Walpole was more like a sprite than a man. And how can poor flesh and blood mortals be expected wholly to understand a sprite?

Perhaps it is impossible to love one either. Horace Walpole is not exactly lovable. But he is wonderful. Never was anyone born with a greater talent for living. For he combined, in a most unusual way, the gusto and curiosity needed to enjoy life with the judgment and self-discipline required to regulate it: so that—and this is the secret of successful living—he never wasted a moment doing anything for which he was unfitted. Perceiving precisely where his taste and capacities lay, he constructed his scheme of existence rigidly within the limits revealed by this perception. Like his letters, his life was a conscious work of art. And since it was executed with an unflagging spirit and an incomparable sense of style, it was, of its kind, a masterpiece. Even now, a hundred and sixty years after his death, and when his personality can only communicate itself to us through the cold medium of print, we enjoy the spectacle of Horace Walpole, as we enjoy a perfect performance of some Mozartian aria. "Que voulez-vous?" says the wise Lemaître. "La perfection absolue fait toujours plaisir."

It pleased Gray all right. Walpole's easy good breeding, his charming rococo airs were just the things to fascinate him, especially since he can never have come across them before. On his side Gray had something to offer Walpole. Aristocratic circles, however polished, tend to be philistine. Walpole was unlikely to have met anyone at home to whom the life

of art and imagination was the precious thing it was to Gray.
He was also far too clever to be put off by Gray's superficial
awkwardness of manner. Never indeed was Walpole's easy
mastery of the art of living more evident than in the inde-
pendent track he cut calmly for himself through the rough and
tumble of Eton life. That rough and tumble appealed to
him as little as it did to Gray. He was too grown-up, as well
as too unathletic. "I can reflect with great joy," he wrote to a
friend during the holidays when he was fourteen years old,
"on the moments we passed together at Eton; and long to
talk 'em over, as I think we could recollect a dozen passages
which were something above the common run of schoolboys'
diversions. I can remember with no small satisfaction we
did not pass our time in gloriously beating great clowns. . . .
We had other amusements."

Neither did Walpole work very hard at his lessons. Culture
in his view was meant to be a pleasure, not a form of hard
labour. If his tutor set him any task extra to the regular
requirements of the curriculum, he would make a point of
not getting it done. "What, learn more than I am absolutely
forced to learn!" he exclaimed in comic horror. These dusty
pedagogues must, he felt, be made to realize that Sir Robert
Walpole's son was not to be bullied. Instead he spent his time
reading poems and romances, and still more in talking to his
friends. He made a great many of these, more than Gray was
able to do. Gay, gossipy, and not at all shy, he loved company:
and the fact that, unlike Gray, he came from the same patrician
background as the majority of his schoolfellows gave him
more in common with them. With those of them who
seemed to be sufficiently civilized to be possible companions,
he was amused to discuss the events of the world, of politics
and fashion, from which they all sprang. Still, these friends
had nothing to offer to the artist in Walpole. To satisfy this
he struck up with Gray and West. The more they saw of

each other, the more they proved to have in common. Soon they were inseparable.

To the trio a fourth attached himself, Thomas Ashton. He was not much of an addition; a smug-faced ungainly boy, clever enough at his books but with none of the others' genuine sensibility. Moreover he was intriguing and pushing, rather too well aware of the future advantages to be gathered by making friends with the Prime Minister's son. He took pains to acquire the conversational tone of the group. He did not do it very well, but well enough to succeed in his aim. Boys— even boys like Gray and Walpole—seldom pause to examine the motives of those who take pains to make themselves pleasant to them. The trio became a quartet. Children are ritualists delighting in formal ranks and titles. As less sophisticated boys enjoy belonging to gangs and secret societies with names like the "Hidden Hand", so these christened their association "the Quadruple Alliance". Each member had a nickname taken from the stories they read, and the plays they acted together. Gray was Orozamades, Ashton, Almanzor, West, Zephyrus and Walpole, Celadon.

The names are romantic. Indeed the spirit that animated the Quadruple Alliance was extremely romantic, in the mild and artificial sense in which the eighteenth century understood the word.

"Were not the playing fields of Eton food for all manner of flights?" wrote Walpole some years later. "No old maid's gown, though it had been tormented into all the fashions from King James to King George ever underwent so many transformations as those poor plains have in my idea. At first I was contented with tending a visionary flock, and sighing some pastorial name to the echo of the cascade under the bridge. How happy should I have been to have had a kingdom only for the pleasure of being driven from it, and living disguised in an humble vale! As I got further into Virgil and Clelia, I found myself transported from Arcadia to the garden of Italy; and saw Windsor Castle in no other view than the *Capitoli immobile saxum*. I wish a committee of the House of Commons may ever seem to be the senate; or a bill appear half so agreeable as a billet-doux. You see how deep you have carried me into old stories; I write of them with pleasure, but shall talk of them with more to you. I can't say I am sorry I was never quite a school-boy: an expedition against barge-men, or a match at cricket, may be very pretty things to recollect; but, thank my stars, I can remember things that are very near as pretty."

They all indulged in similar fancies. Shepherds, knights errant, disguised princesses filled their thoughts. They read Spenser, Milton, Shakespeare, with passionate enthusiasm. From each book new figures arose to throng their day-dreams.

Their affection for each other was romantic, too. School-boys' affections tend to be. In them the capacity for love awakens, and, as it were, tries out its paces. Nor in the eighteenth century were such feelings inhibited by the fear of being thought silly or unmanly. Even to one of his less poetic friends Walpole could write: "My dearest Charles, I find we not only sympathise in the tenderest friendship for one another, but also in the result of that which is the jealousy you mention."

In the atmosphere of the Quadruple Alliance, the emotional temperature was, as it might be expected, yet higher. Walpole and West, Gray and Ashton saw themselves as Damon and Pythias, Orestes and Pylades, inheritors of the glorious tradition of antique comradeship, united to one another by a refined affinity of soul beyond the reach of commonplace persons. Carefully tended, as on some classical altar, the flame of sentimental friendship gave light and warmth to their fastidious existences. They yielded themselves with rapture to its ardours and tendernesses: and they expressed them with a stilted elaboration which is a trifle absurd. Indeed there is something absurd about the Quadruple Alliance, with its pretences of maturity, its mincing graces. But it was also charming. The spectacle of children playing at being grown up always has charm. Moreover, these particular children did it so prettily. The exaggerations of their youthful affectations did not conceal the fact that they were possessed of an unusual sensibility and feeling for style. These demure boys performing their florid minuet of fancy and sentiment, amid the lawns and moss-grown cloisters of the ancient school present a picture of Watteaulike delicacy, all the more piquant for the contrast between the artificial formality of the dance, and the youthful freshness of the dancers.

Nor did they take themselves so seriously as to be over-solemn. In Gray and Walpole at any rate, the sense of comedy was quite as acute as the poetic sense. They enjoyed reading about Lady Wishfort and Falstaff as much as about Hamlet and Dido: and themselves they exercised their growing wits in mocking, not without pride in their own intellectual superiority, at the dolts and fools around them. Moreover, unboyish though they might be in many respects, they had a boyish love of pure fun. They delighted in comic nicknames, innocent coarsenesses, private jokes endlessly repeated, but always with renewed pleasure: their gravest talks were liable to be suddenly interrupted by flights of exuberant nonsense, fits of delicious uncontrollable giggles.

They were happy. To Gray indeed, looking back in later years, these days seemed the happiest of his life. Men are apt to think this, when reflecting sentimentally on their school days. In his case, however, it seems likely to have been true.

At Eton he had discovered for the first time, and glowing all the brighter by contrast with his unhappy home, an existence centred on those pleasures of literature and friendship for which his nature instinctively craved. Its monastic seclusion protected him from the rough world, and he was still too young to worry about the future. Moreover, his actual capacity for enjoying himself was greater than it was ever to be again. For he was of that sensitive, un-vital type, in whom high spirits evaporate with boyhood.

Certainly it was a delightful existence. But it was not to last. By 1735 Gray had grown into a man, and must enter the world. Superficially at any rate, he was ready for it. People grew up much earlier in those days. Gray and his friends were precocious even for the period. By eighteen, the Quadruple Alliance—to judge by the letters they wrote to one another— were as advanced as young men of twenty-three are to-day. Not only did they express themselves with a self-assured ease, unmarked by a trace of clumsiness or naïveté, but they had matured into a coherent social group, with its own character- istic manner, its own characteristic outlook. The manner was formal and Frenchified, full of gesture and compliment, graceful gush, and ornate flourishes of wit and fancy. The outlook was aesthetic. The Quadruple Alliance loved to cultivate the finer pleasures of taste and sentiment. If they were in a serious mood they talked of literature and the opera: if frivolous, they gossiped about personalities and fashions. Even when they turned their attention for a moment to history or natural science, the motive was aesthetic. These things appealed in some way to their imagination or sense of beauty. Strenuous intellectual questionings attracted them as little as sport or practical business. There is no arguing in the letters. The Quadruple Alliance was dedicated to the service of the Muses and the Graces.

So far its members were like aesthetic young men in any

period: but the fact that they were children of the eighteenth century, the rational, worldly-wise eighteenth century, made them strikingly different from the Paterian aesthete of a later age. They did not go in for eccentricity or ecstasy; their manners, though flowery, were not unconventional; and their culture was no soul adventure into regions of strange beauty, but a lucid, sensible affair of good taste and good scholarship. "What was the correct diction for an epic?" they asked each other. "How should one interpret some difficult passage of Ovid or Tibullus?" Nor did art inspire them with mystical feelings. "Poetry is the most enchanting thing in the world," said West. His friends would have agreed with him: but they meant that it was the most exquisite of pleasures, not the revelation of a spiritual mystery. As for rhapsodizing about it after the fashion of the Paterian aesthete, the Quadruple Alliance would have thought such a thing ridiculous. Their sense of comedy was far too strong. Even when they were talking about the subjects they loved best, their characteristic tone was a light, urbane, irony. This lightness was encouraged by the fact that there was a strain of the man-of-the-world in the ideal they set up for themselves. Provinciality and rusticity disgusted them: they admired sophistication and elegance. And sophistication and elegance implied a certain airy flippancy of tone that excluded the possibility of rapture. Here we may detect the influence of Walpole on the group. Its mental atmosphere was a blend of the spirit of Gray on the one hand, and of Walpole on the other. The interests that bound them together were Gray's: but the tone in which they discussed them was Walpole's. Walpole, with his dazzling aura of fashion inevitably set the standard of style for his humbler friends. He affected them all the more because concern for style was the outstanding characteristic of the group. Orthodox enough in their opinions, the members of the Quadruple Alliance differed from the average in the elaborate refinement with which they sought to present them to the world.

They succeeded in their aim. No young men can ever have been more exquisitely civilized. Perhaps too civilized. The Quadruple Alliance, it must be owned, were mannered, finnicky, hard to please, and unspontaneous. Deliberate stylishness inhibits spontaneity. Even with each other they could not relax in a homely friendliness. However, they did not want to. Homely friendliness was not at all the sort of thing that appealed to their taste. Besides, they enjoyed showing off to each other; and being shown off to, as well. They were enthusiastic about each other's talents, and like other coteries of clever young men they took pleasure in thinking that they formed a front; that they stood for civilization against the hordes of barbarians and philistines, of uncouth pedants, and hard-drinking hallooing hunting men, of which the world seemed so largely and so regrettably composed; and in whose company they felt as comfortable as four cats among a pack of dogs. Not that they wanted to enter into combat with them. Cats do not attack dogs. With a shudder of delicate ironic horror, the Quadruple Alliance preferred to turn their backs on the displeasing spectacle of average mankind, and to seek solace in the delights of each other's society.

Unfortunately Fate did not permit them to do this for very long. In October, 1734, West left Eton for Oxford, and Ashton and Gray for Cambridge; Walpole followed them there six months later. His life, however, soon began to develop on lines which made the close, continuous association of Eton days impossible. Aristocratic young men in the eighteenth century took their University careers very lightly. They came and went as they felt inclined; though they sometimes did a little leisurely reading in some author who took their fancy, they seldom embarked on a regular course of study: and hardly ever bothered to take a degree. Walpole, launched for the first time as a grown-up young man into the intoxicating world of London social life, appeared at Cambridge only occasionally. Gray missed him very much. His first years at the University were not happy. It was not only that he felt cut off from his former friends. He was also very poor. £20 a year in scholarships, and with the little his mother could save from the depredations of her husband, was all he had to live on. Though he practised a rigid economy, it was enough. Unluckily, too, he was the type of character who minds poverty particularly acutely. It intensified his nervous anxiety about the future, and it made him feel dependent on circumstances in a way that outraged his pride. Moreover his temperament desired those graces and elegancies of living which, alas, are not to be had without money. These four years left him for the rest of his life possessed by a sense of the necessity of financial independence.

Further, he did not at first take to Cambridge. This is hardly to be wondered at. An English University of the time was no place for the civilized spirit, as Gibbon was to find forty years later. Cambridge, when Gray went there, was a stagnant backwater, cut off from the flowing mainstream of contemporary culture, a sort of stuffy, unspiritual monastery, ruled over by an inert mass of stodgy celibates—how smugly their bewigged countenances still stare down at us from the panelled walls of combination rooms—who, having risen from narrow circumstances to achieve their Fellowships, had relaxed for the rest of their lives into a monotonous existence of over-eating, over-drinking, and petty College business. Now and again a distinguished scholar appeared among them. But for the most part, their intellectual standards were low. Promotion went by patronage; so that a man might be made a Professor in a subject he knew nothing about, just because he had known how to flatter and pull strings in the right quarter. As for the ordinary College tutor, he was often an idle, ignorant man, who scarcely bothered to see his pupils more than twice in the term. Fancy, thought Gray, being put under the direction of a drunken illiterate like Mr. Birkett! As a matter of fact, even if he had approved of Mr. Birkett, Gray would not have much enjoyed working under him. For he found the curriculum uninspiring; a dry old-fashioned logic-chopping affair, involving a good deal of mathematics and metaphysics, and with nothing in it to appeal to the poetic spirit. "Must I plunge into metaphysics?" he complained to West. "Alas, I cannot see in the dark: nature has not furnished me with the optics of a cat. Must I pore upon mathematics? Alas, I cannot see in too much light: I am no eagle. It is very possible that two and two make four, but I would not give four farthings to demonstrate this ever so clearly: and if these be the profits of life, give me the amusements of it."

Nor did the company of his fellow students offer much compensation for the deficiencies of the dons and the curriculum. Undergraduates were divided mainly into two classes. Of these, the scions of the aristocracy occupied such time as they spent at Cambridge in racing by day, and by night revelling round the streets, breaking the heads of unoffending townsmen: while the rest—dons and country parsons in embryo—sat about in an atmosphere of beer and tobacco smoke, exchanging trivial gossip, and ponderous jokes. Gray was too poor to associate with the aristocrats, even had he wanted to. Now and again, however, he was drawn into the company of the others. In a letter to Walpole he expatiates on his sufferings there.

"Do but imagine me pent up in a room hired for the purpose, and none of the largest, from 7 o'clock at night, till 4 in the morning! 'midst hogheads of liquor and quantities of tobacco, surrounded by 30 of these creatures, infinitely below the meanest people you could ever form an idea of; toasting bawdy healths and deafened with their unmeaning roar; Jesus! but I must tell you of a fat mortal who stuck close to me. . . . Well! he was so maudlin and so loving, and told me long stories interrupted by the sourest interjections, with moral discourses upon God knows what; I was almost drunk too. . . . You will think it a strange compliment when I tell you how often I thought of you, all the while: but will forgive me when you recollect that it was a great piece of philosophy in me to be able, in the midst of noise and disturbance, to call to mind the most agreeable thing in the world."

As was to be expected in these circumstances, Gray spent most of his time by himself; musing his way through the streets to lectures under the low-lying Cambridge sky, or in the ancient quiet of his College rooms, reading, learning Italian, and playing toccatas and sarabands on the pianoforte. It does not sound such an unsuitable life for him in its minor-key way. After all, his occupations were congenial; he liked learning Italian and playing the pianoforte. Indeed, these particular years, too, turned out profitable to his mental development. Their very emptiness gave him room to cultivate those aesthetic and literary interests in which his creative impulse was to find fulfilment: their very silence enabled him to listen more attentively to the immaterial voices of the mighty dead, of Milton and Tasso, Horace and Racine, Spenser and Mme de Sevigné. For he soaked himself in the literature of many ages and nations. Under their enriching influence his taste refined itself, his imaginative life acquired shape, strength, amplitude.

Nor was it as if he felt more at home in other places; amid the sordid quarrellings of his Mother's house in Cornhill, or

99

staying with his sporting Uncle at Burnham Beeches—an object of contempt, because he read and walked when he could have been out with the hounds, and where he was forced to write his letters standing up, because all the chairs were occupied by his Uncle's stinking, barking dogs. Cambridge, with all its defects, was better than this. As the years passed, though he hardly liked to admit it, the place began to get a hold on him. When he got an invitation to go away, he found himself disinclined to accept it. "I don't know how it is, I have a sort of reluctance to leave this place, unamiable as it may seem. It is true Cambridge is very ugly, the Town is very dirty, and very dull, but I am like a cabbage; where I am stuck, I love to grow."

Moreover with the years some of the chief ills which at first he complained of at Cambridge began to disappear. He had contrived, with the help of the despised Mr. Birkett, to persuade the authorities to allow him to give up taking a degree, in spite of the fact that he was receiving a scholarship from them; so that he could now devote himself undisturbed to the studies he liked. And he began to find a few kindred spirits in the place, notably a comfortable, kindly scholarly man called Wharton, and a pleasant, vigorous little scholar named Brown. He managed, too, to keep up his connection with the Quadruple Alliance. Ashton was at Cambridge. And though he seems to have grown steadily less attractive with the years—sedulously planning his career, pompously fussing lest he had unconsciously offended someone who could obstruct his advancement—yet Ashton was an original member of the group with whom one could recall time past, and laugh at the old jokes. With Walpole and West, Gray maintained his connection mainly by letters. Not entirely though; now and again the door of his rooms would open and in flashed Walpole, voluble and intimate as ever, and bubbling over with fascinating news about the newest Italian castrato singer, or the latest scandal in high society. Gray loved hearing about high society, or indeed, about any society. One of his chief pleasures in talking to Walpole arose from the fact that Walpole acted as a link between his friend's solitude and the world, that with Walpole Gray could share vicariously in that easy intercourse with his fellow man which in reality he found so difficult. He enjoyed this the more because it was intercourse in surroundings so agreeable to his imagination. Beauty did not have to be solemn to please Gray. He was very susceptible to the decorative quality in fashionable life, its frills and pretty fopperies, and he had an eye for their details. With what delighted precision does he observe Queen Caroline's costume, watching the opera "in a green velvet sac, embroidered on the facings and sleeves with silver, and a little French cap, and big black hood, and her hair in curls round her face." He was full of the blue and gold feux d'artifices that adorned the new production of Handel's "Atlanta". Walpole was the only one of his friends equally interested in these frivolities. Walpole, too, was the only one who could tell him about them. Routs, balls, masquerades—Gray wanted to hear about everything.

"Thou dear envious Imp," he exclaimed to him, "to set me a longing with accounts of plays and operas, and masquerades, after hearing of which, I can no more think of Logick and stuff, than you could of Divinity at a ball, or of Caudle and Carraway-Comfits after having been stuffed at a Christening: heaven knows! we have nobody in our College that has seen London, but one; and he, I believe, comes out of Vinegar-yard, and looks like toasted Cheshire cheese, strewed with brown Sugar. I beg you, give me the minutest Circumstances of your Diversions and your Indiversions; tho' if it is as great a trouble to you to write, as it is a pleasure to me to get 'em my heart, I fear I shan't hear from you once in a twelvemonth, and dear, now be very punctual and very long."

Indeed absence only served to increase the unique glamour with which, in Gray's eyes, Walpole's figure was irradiated. How wonderful it was to find a friend as fastidious and fussy as himself—Walpole rushes to him for sympathy when he is forced to spend a dreadful week in the sporting atmosphere of his Father's country house—who was yet somehow possessed of the savoir faire and zest for living which he, Gray, longed for and lacked.

"I am sufficiently awake to answer your letter," he told him, "though likely to be more dull than you write in sleep: and indeed I do not believe that you ever are so much asleep, but you can write to a relation, play a sober game of piquet, keep to a tête-à-tête conversation, seal a bargain, or perform any of the little offices of life with tolerable spirit: certain I am there are many people in the world who in their deep spirits are no better awake than you are at four in the morning, reclined upon your pillow."

Of course the very fact that his friend was such a brilliant figure imposed a certain strain in Gray's relations with him. It is to be noted in the foregoing quotation that Gray apologizes for being dull. At all costs he felt he must avoid dullness, if he was to be worthy of Walpole's interest in him. His letters to him now cast in the form of a mock oriental tale, now in that of an epistle from a god-daughter, now interspersed with verses, now expressed in a comic parody of Shakespearean English—are elaborate essays in the art of entertainment; frothy, sparkling confections, in which he has exercised himself to put all his powers of wit and fancy, and

from which anything which might be thought boring is
carefully excluded. Walpole, not unnaturally, accepted the
version of Gray's character thus carefully presented to him.
Humour he took to be Gray's natural mood. His gravity he
dismissed as a mere trick of manner, and his occasional sighs of
melancholy as pardonable affectations.

West was in no danger of falling into this error. For, if
Walpole provided a link between Gray and the outer world,
West was the companion of his inner life. Not that their
relations were without rubs. They met very seldom, not
more than twice in three years. And on one of these occasions
at least, they were too shy to feel completely easy with one
another. "West sup'd with me the night before I came out of
town," Gray related; "we both fancied at first we had a great
many things to say to one another; but when it came to the
push, I found, I had forgot all I intended to say, and he stood
upon Punctilios and would not speak first, and so we parted."
There is a caustic truthfulness about this account which is a
little formidable. It was characteristic of Gray though.
Critical and insecure, he was always, as it were, taking the
temperature of his friendships to see if they were providing
the requisite warmth and light. If they were not, he was not
the man to try and hide it from himself. However, the
affection between him and West was too deep to be impaired
by one awkward interview. Within a month he is writing
to him as affectionately as ever. Though Gray always tries
to be agreeable, his letters to West were both franker and
graver than those to Walpole. He writes a great deal about
scholarship and literature, sends verses for West's criticism,
or comments on verses West has sent to him. Together they
lamented the aridness of intellectual life at their respective
Universities. "Sure it was of this place now Cambridge,"
exclaimed Gray, "but formerly known as Babylon, that the
prophet spoke when he said 'that the wild beasts of the forests

shall dwell there, and their houses shall be full of doleful
creatures'." To West Gray allowed himself to betray his
troubled mind, as he could not do to Walpole: and now and
again the emotional tone deepened as with a charming, shy
smile, Gray revealed that he was writing to one of the very few
human beings he loved. "As the most undeserving people
in the world most often have the vanity to wish somebody had
a regard for them, so I need not wonder at my own in being
pleased that you care about me. You need not doubt, therefore, of having a first row in the front box of my little heart,
and I believe that you are in no danger of being crowded
there."

West responded ardently to these declarations. Unlike his
friends, he was unreserved: and he was touchingly pleased to
find that anyone cared for him. Since leaving Eton, his life
had been even drearier than Gray's. He had no old friends at
all at Oxford, and he shrank too much from the novelty of
making new ones. Besides, he was a tenderer plant than
Gray. There was nothing in him of that fundamental self-
discipline and solidity of mind that enabled Gray to construct
a life of fruitful study out of the loneliness of Cambridge.
Wretched health—West was a victim of acute attacks of
headache, which, while they lasted, prostrated him completely—had increased the natural weakness of a disposition
high strung, unconcentrated and the prey to waves of black
despair, in which joy, youth, life itself, seemed to be slipping
through his nerveless fingers, gleaming and insubstantial as
the waters of a stream. He could not bring himself to get
down to any regular work. Only as he wandered forlornly
by the willows and fritillaries of Addison's Walk, brooding
endlessly over those Eton days when alone he had been
happy, while Magdalen Tower chimed out the melancholy
hours overhead, his over-burdened heart sighed itself forth
in a strain of elegiac sadness.

Saint of this learned awful grove,
While slow along thy walks I rove,
The pleasing scene, which all that see
   Admire, is lost to me.

The thought, which still my breast invades,
Nigh yonder springs, nigh yonder shades,
Still, as I pass, the memory brings
   Of sweeter shades and springs.

Lost and inwrapt in thought profound,
Absent I tread Etonian ground;
Then starting from the dear mistake,
   As disenchanted, wake.

What though from sorrow free, at best
I'm thus but negatively blest:
Yet still, I find, true joy I miss:
   True joy's a social bliss.

Oh! How I long again with those,
Whom first my boyish heart had chose,
Together through the friendly shade
   To stray, as once I stray'd!

Their presence would the scene endear
Like paradise would all appear,
More sweet around the flowers would blow,
   More soft the waters flow.

No wonder he was grateful to Gray, when he said he loved him. "I singled you out for a friend," West cried passionately, "and I would have you know me to be yours, if you deem me worthy—alas Gray, you cannot imagine how miserably my time passes away; my health and nerves and spirits are, I thank my stars, the very worst in Oxford . . . give me leave to say I find no physic comparable to your letters."

Gray could sympathize with West's lamentations. His own feelings were, at times, all too similar. Since leaving school his own prevailing mood had been a melancholy one. It was nothing like so acute as West's. Ennui, a sense of emptiness, apathy, a sort of greyness of the spirit which prevented him enjoying anything completely, were its characteristics. "When you have seen one of my days," he writes, "you have seen a whole year of my life. They go round and round like a blind horse in the mill, only he has the satisfaction of fancying he makes progress, and gets some ground: my eyes are open enough to see the same dull prospect, and having made four and twenty steps more, I shall now be just where I was." And again, "low spirits are my true and faithful companions. They get up with me, go to bed with me, make journeys and returns as I do; nay, and pay visits, and will even affect to be jocose, and share a feeble laugh with me, but most commonly we are alone together, and are the prettiest, insipid company in the world."

The origin of this melancholy of Gray's is to be found partly in a constitutional languor of temperament, partly in that fundamental suspicion of life engendered in him by too early an acquaintance with its power to hurt. Latent during his school days, it was bound to make itself felt when he was first as a man compelled to confront the world. The world—it loomed up before his troubled, adolescent gaze, a bewildering, dangerous place, in which his shrinking spirit felt incurably alien. His mode of life did nothing to reconcile him to it. Poverty and solitude encourage despondency: the monastic seclusion in which he lived made him shyer than ever. Why did he feel disinclined to leave Cambridge, since he found it so dull? Because leaving it meant venturing into a hostile region, where nothing was to be had which he felt worth winning. Instead he devoted himself to study. This, as we have seen, was good for him: in it, the intellectual half of his nature found fulfilment; this was why he was not as unhappy as West. But he was not sufficiently impersonal to be completely satisfied by intellectual activity. He needed the sweetness of human contact, he needed love. If he had been a normal young man he would, at this stage in his development, have fallen in love. But Gray was very far from being a normal young man. Stiff and academic, he was embarrassed in the company of young women, checked by what he felt to be his lack of worldly polish. He could not bear to imagine himself taking part in any love affair, unless it was conducted with elegant ease. And how in the world was he, of all people, to acquire elegant ease? When Walpole wrote to tell him about an amorous intrigue in which he was engaged, Gray replied, with a forced jauntiness of tone, which ill concealed his painful sense of inferiority, that he had sometimes considered embarking on a similar adventure himself, but that he had, in the end, come to the conclusion that he was not equipped for it.

"Would you believe it, 'tis the very thing I would wish to apply to myself. Ay! as simply as I stand here. But then the apparatus necessary to it calls for so much; nay, a part of it is wholly out of one's power to procure. Then who should pare one, and burnish one? For they would have more trouble and fuss with me than Cinderaxa's sisters had with their feet to make 'em fit for the little glass slipper. Oh yes! to be sure, one must be licked; now to lick oneself I take altogether impracticable, and to ask another to lick one, would not be quite so civil. Bear I was born, and bear I believe I am likely to remain."

Gray was further inhibited in these matters by the fact that relations with a woman meant adventure, meant plunging into that risky, earthy world of adult manhood, where he felt so out of place. Nor was it natural for him to take the masculine and dominant rôle expected in such a relationship. Native temperament and childish experience had combined to make him neither dominant nor masculine where his personal emotions were concerned. In consequence of all this, his capacity for romantic sentiment tended to be diverted into his feeling for his old friends, for West and Walpole. These feelings, though deep and productive at moments of an exquisite happiness, could not fully satisfy the needs of his heart. The relationships involved in them were careful, delicate, precarious affairs of rarefied sentiment and subtle intellectual sympathies, liable to be disturbed by the slightest breath of discord, and quite unable either to bring him down to earth, or to dispel his sense of insecurity. His suspicion of life remained, and with it his lack of spirits.

It was in no sanguine mood, therefore, that in September, 1738, Gray packed his boxes to leave Cambridge. He had to go; if he was ever to mend his wordly fortunes, he must take up a profession. But what profession? Unenthusiastically he considered the Bar. West was thinking of this too. Perhaps they might make a start together. Even so Gray did not find the prospect exhilarating. However, before anything was fixed, something happened which changed his plans entirely. Sir Robert Walpole, in accordance with Whig tradition, was sending Walpole abroad to finish his education by a protracted grand tour of the Continent. Now Walpole wrote and asked Gray to come with him as his guest. There could be no question of a refusal. To see with his own eyes all the historical places and famous works of art, which for so many years had filled his imagination; to see them in the company of dearest Celadon, and on a journey where he would travel in the greatest possible comfort—this was a chance not to be missed. At the end of March, 1739, the two young men were across the Channel. They were not back again till 1741.

This two years' sojourn abroad was a unique adventure in Gray's retired life. It was also decisive in shaping his subsequent character and career. All this makes it the more irritating that, as usual with Gray, we do not know enough about it. Not that he is silent on the subject. Page after page scored over with his scholarly handwriting arrived regularly in England by every postbag. But, as always, there is a great deal that these pages do not tell us. Gray's barrier of gentlemanly reserve interposes itself between us and intimate confession: and it is rendered more tantalizingly effective by the fact that he was so interested in the sights he saw, that he devotes a large part of his space to describing them in detail, instead of telling us about himself. Like many cultured travellers, Gray tended to confuse a good letter with a good guide-book. The result is that the journey passes before our mental eye rather like a cinema film of which we do not catch all the words. Vividly we see the contrasting figures of the two young men—Gray's short, neat, and prim, Walpole's slim, vivacious and modish—as they stepped their delicate way through an ever-changing succession of varied, multi-coloured scenes, Louis XV's Paris, Alpine crags and torrents, the masques and torch-light of the Florentine carnival, the crumbling magnificence of baroque Rome, the ruins and sunset distances of the Campagna. But we have to guess at the ebb and flow of feelings which animated them during their progress; mainly by hints do we follow the course of the drama of which this picturesque background was the setting. For it was a drama: an entertaining, distressing little tragi-comedy of old friendship exposed to new strains, wearing thinner and thinner under their pressure, till, with a painful, resounding snap, it breaks.

The strains were inevitable. Travelling abroad is notoriously a hard test for any friendship. At home friends meet when they feel inclined, and on common ground, where only those sides in them which are sympathetic are apparent. Abroad they are together all the time, whether they feel like it or not. Worst still, they are forced to know each other completely; each is brought face to face with those aspects of his friend's character with which he has no particular affinity. More often than not he finds them intolerably jarring. So it was with Gray and Walpole. Their friendship had grown up at Eton and Cambridge, where they were drawn together by the fact that they both liked art and literature, and both disliked athletics and rough boys. In some other respects not so apparent at school, they were very different. Walpole was a born gay citizen of the world, to whom the things of the mind and imagination, keenly as he enjoyed them, came second to the pleasures of social life. Gray, on the other hand, was a pensive recluse, with neither taste nor talent for social pleasures, to whom the things of the mind and imagination were the centre of existence, the source of all his most precious and memorable experiences. Up to now these differences, in so far as they were aware of them, only added to the charm each found in the other. Gray, as we have seen, was exhilarated by the whiff of fashion that blew from Walpole: Walpole enjoyed savouring the atmosphere of cloistered contemplation which floated round Gray. When they were living together, however, and had, in practice, to adjust their lives to one another, these differences were bound to cause trouble. All the more when they were accentuated by the differences in their social positions. Here was another source of friction discovered by their journey. In the democracy of school and college, Gray and Walpole had been on equal terms. Out in the world, and more especially in that world of cosmopolitan high society into which Walpole inevitably went, a gulf disclosed itself. Walpole was the son of the rich Prime Minister of England; Gray was the insignificant child of a warehouse keeper, only admitted into these exalted circles because he was Walpole's friend. To anyone nervously proud as he was, this must produce a painful sense of inferiority. It was not diminished by the fact that he knew, and Walpole knew, that Walpole was paying for him.

Of course, if they had been outstandingly easy-going, or outstandingly insensitive, they might have got on in spite of these causes of ill feeling. But Gray and Walpole were neither of them easy-going or insensitive. It was not in either to let things slide, or to take the rough with the smooth. On the contrary, they were a touchy, huffy, critical pair, quickly irritated, quickly bored, agonizingly conscious of every shade in each other's moods, and sharp to detect any failings in another person, however fond they might be of him. In addition, Walpole had much of the easy inconsiderateness and unconscious arrogance of the young patrician that he was; while Gray suffered from a middle-class readiness to suspect slights and then take solemn offence at them. Altogether it would have been a miracle if they had managed to get through their journey without serious trouble.

It took some time in coming, however. They started off under a cloudless sky. Indeed, on the eve of departure, Walpole was seized with such an ardent impulse of affection for his dear Orozmades, that he made a will bequeathing to him everything of which he might die possessed. And for the next nine months, in spite of an occasional rub, they seemed to have got on pretty well. Gray, it is true, so Walpole recalled later, had shown he could be tiresome as early as their arrival at Calais. He had persisted in feeling sick on a calm sea. This was soon forgotten, however, in the intoxicating excitement both felt at being abroad for the first time. Bowling along in their post-chaise, they gazed out of the windows, delightedly noting each detail in which the French scene differed from the English. The methodical Gray began keeping a journal in which he carefully described any object which struck him as of particular interest. Characteristically these objects were nearly always inanimate; landscape and historical monuments, not people. They made their first protracted stay in Paris. There their zest for sight-seeing remained undiminished. They visited Versailles—very disappointing they thought it, with its pompous, trivial façade and childish waterworks—Trianon, Nôtre Dame, the theatre, the opera. They also bought some new clothes. Gray, who was interested in his own clothes, as well as those of other people, had himself got up in the height of French fashion, tight silk breeches, a muff, and hair powdered and curled "en Bequille". He enjoyed his new appearance; he enjoyed Paris altogether. There was so much to see, he said, that he was quite happy walking about the streets. However, his enjoyment of Paris was qualified by a faint shadow of storms to come. Paris with Walpole meant social life. They were invited to parties. It is possible that Gray fancied he might enjoy them. What with his silk breeches and his muff, perhaps he might not feel himself "a bear" any longer. If he did cherish any such idea, he seems to have been soon disappointed. We remark that he often remains at home in the evening when Walpole is out, also that Walpole, if he does stay in, complains of finding the evening a little flat. Not indeed that he enjoyed going out very much either. French society turned out to take little interest in young foreigners, unless it could gain some practical profit from them, by winning their money at cards. Walpole did not care for cards; he was therefore driven for company to the English Colony. It hardly seemed worth coming abroad for this. Perhaps, after all, it was better to stay at home with Gray. Certainly it was, when their party was enlarged by the arrival of Walpole's

charming young cousin, Henry Conway, who had been
sent to France to learn the language. The three young men
got on extremely well; so well that Walpole and Gray were
persuaded by Conway to change their plans and accompany
him to Rheims, where he was to spend the summer. Rheims,
a quiet provincial town, whose social life was ruled over by a
stiff little group of local nobility and garrison officers, was
not the place to seduce Walpole from Gray's side. One
evening, indeed, it did brighten up. Some ladies and gentlemen had met together to walk in someone's garden; inspired
by Walpole's indefatigable party spirit, the sober gathering
suddenly blossomed into a graceful Lancret-like fête cham-
pêtre. Supper was called for and spread in the open air by a
murmuring fountain; after supper came songs; after songs,
dancing. With their silks and satins gleaming shadowy in the
July moonlight, the company swam and tripped through
minuet and country dance, till at five in the morning, the
violins still playing before them, they capered their way
through the sleeping streets, to bed. Encouraged by the
success of this impromptu festivity, Walpole proposed giving
a ball. But Rheims society, after this unprecedented outburst,
had sunk back into its customary languor, and the scheme fell
through. For the rest of their stay, the young men had to
entertain themselves by reading and talking to each other.
Gray found nothing to complain of in such a mode of life.

He had still less to complain of in the next phase of his
travel. Starting in September, for two months he and
Walpole wended their way through Burgundy, Savoy and
Switzerland, to Italy; a leisurely, discursive, enchanting
journey, made romantic by a thousand glimpses of vineyard
and mountain gorge, abbey and ruined castle, the tombs of the
Burgundian kings near Dijon, the shining levels of the Lake
of Leman, sublime Alpine vistas, culminating in the wild St.
Gothard Pass—masked and muffled in fur, they were carried

across it in the snow by sturdy mountaineers—and then the gradual descent into the olives and autumnal sunshine of the Italian plain. The peaks and passes of the high Alps were a trifle too alarming for the cautious Gray to take much pleasure in them—"They carried the permission mountains have of being frightful, rather too far", he said—but otherwise he found himself deeply stirred by mountain scenery. Here he was a pioneer in taste. Only a few years before travellers turned from such "horrid" sights in disgust. But by 1739, imaginative spirits were beginning to find the order and rationality which eighteenth-century civilization imposed on the world, disagreeably cramping and prosaic; and they turned in reaction to seek nourishment for their day-dreams in the savage and the "Gothick". None more than Gray. Even at Eton he had delighted in romance and fairy tale. Since then, in his Cambridge solitude he had fed his fancy on Spenser and mediaeval history. And now here in the flesh were the scenes exactly like those he had dwelt on so often in imagination. It was too good to be true. The precipitous scenery around the Grande Chartreuse impressed him especially; so it did Walpole. They responded to it, however, differently. Walpole enjoyed it simply as a spectacle, the natural counterpart, as it were, to the finest stage scenery imaginable.

"But the road, West, the road! winding round a prodigious mountain and surrounded with others, all shagged with hanging woods, obscured with pines or lost in clouds! Below a torrent breaking through cliffs, and tumbling through fragments of rocks! Sheets of cascades forcing their silver speed down channelled precipices, and hasting into the roughened river at the bottom! Now and then an old foot-bridge, with a broken rail, a leaning cross, a cottage, or the ruin of an hermitage! This sounds too bombast and too romantic to one that has not seen it, too cold for one that has."

Gray, less observant of the picturesque surface, was far more profoundly moved. To him the sight was a landmark in his life, a momentous experience, revealing, as in an awe-inspiring flash, the spiritual nature of the universe.

"In our little journey up to the Grande Chartreuse, I do not remember to have gone ten paces without an exclamation that there was no restraining: not a precipice, not a torrent, not a cliff, but is pregnant with religion and poetry. There are certain scenes that would awe an atheist into belief, without the help of other argument. One need not have a very fantastic imagination to see spirits there at noon-day: you have Death perpetually before your eyes, only so far removed, as to compose the mind without frighting it. I am well persuaded St. Bruno was a man of no common genius, to choose such a situation for retire-ment; and perhaps should have been a disciple of his, had I been born in his time."

A life of seclusion spent in surroundings as spirit-stirring as these—that would have been delightful indeed.

Nothing in Italy roused this sort of emotion in him. But he got a great deal out of Italy, too. If the Chartreuse had made him realize, for the first time, the full power of nature to move the soul, Italy made him realize the full power of art. Genoa with its marble palaces, gleaming white against the sapphire of the Mediterranean, the Correggios at Palma, the colonnaded streets of Bologna, his first sight of the towers of Florence rising pearly through the mists of an October evening—each had its contribution to make to his growing store of exquisite and fertilizing impressions.

At Florence they were welcomed by the Minister, Sir
Horace Mann. He turned out to be a very sympathetic
personality: a fastidious, invalidish bachelor of thirty-eight,
extremely intelligent, and with an affected manner. Delighted
to find such kindred spirits after the dreary horde of loutish
English youths, bear-led by pedantic parsons, who made up
the greater part of English visitors to Florence, and pleased
also that one of these kindred spirits should be the son of
the Prime Minister, Mann pressed them to make a long stay.
They were quite willing. Walpole was tired of bad inns and
jolting journeys, and Gray wanted time thoroughly to study
the antiquities of the place. For the next few months they
were settled at Florence. With their establishment there, a
new phase opened in their journey. Walpole was responsible
for it. By this time he had begun to discover that he could
have a great deal too much of sightseeing.

"A force d'en avoir vu, I have left off screaming, Lord!
this! and Lord! that! To speak sincerely, Calais surprised
me more than anything I have seen since. I recollect the
joy I used to propose if I could but once see the Great
Duke's gallery; I walk into it now with as little emotion
as I should into St. Paul's. The statues are a congregation of
good sort of people, that I have a great deal of unruffled
regard for. The farther I travel, the less I wonder at
anything."

His appetite for social life, on the other hand, was still far
from satisfied. From this point of view Paris and Rheims
had proved disappointing. His first impressions of Florence
were hardly more promising. It seemed just another provincial capital, and the society there, though more pleasure-
loving and informal than that of Rheims, was equally
monotonous.

"Men are so much the same everywhere," he told West, with all the blaséness of his twenty years, "that one scarce perceives any change of situation. The same weaknesses, the same passions, that in England plunge men into elections, drinking, whoring, exist here, and show themselves in the shapes of Jesuits, Cicisbeos, and Corydon ardebat Alexins. . . . Thus child, 'tis dull dealing here!"

However, as time passed, Walpole began to find himself liking Florence better. The people might not be so varied as those in London, but their manners were better, and their mode of living more agreeable. If you felt a desire for culture, why, there were the most famous museums in Europe at your door: otherwise you could relax at pleasant little parties in palaces, or saunters in the Boboli gardens, or in delightful hours spent with Mann over a cup of coffee—admirable Mann disliked strong drink as much as Walpole did—talking about the latest social and political news. Walpole was sufficiently the son of the Prime Minister to enjoy a chance to be in touch with active politics again. The fact that he was the son of the Prime Minister was an advantage to him in Florentine society. Everyone was out to please him, never had he been so appreciated. This naturally made him like Florence better and better.

With the coming of Carnival in 1741, liking warmed to enthusiasm. His youthful capacity for gaiety had not had much opportunity to gratify itself since he came abroad. Dammed up for so long, it now poured itself forth with a foaming irresistible rush into the festivities of the Carnival.

"Well, West," he chatters, "I have found a little unmasked moment to write to you; but for this week past, I have been so muffled up in my domino that I have not had the command of my elbows. But what have you been doing all the morning? Could you not write then? Then I was masked too; I have done nothing but hop out of my domino into bed, and out of bed into my domino. The end of the Carnival is frantic and bacchanalian; all the morn one makes parties in masks to the shops and coffee houses, and all the evening to the operas and balls. Then I have danced, *good gods*, how have I danced! . . . there are but three days more. The two last are to have balls all the morning at the fine, unfinished palace of the Strozzi; and on Tuesday night, a masquerade after supper."

Days and nights like this—ah, surely they were worth a hundred spent staring at mouldering abbeys, and broken-nosed statues!

Gray did not think so. Carnivals were not for him. He was born a trifle middle-aged, and he felt as embarrassed as ever in the company of strangers. Closer acquaintance with society had only served to prove to him that he was unfitted for it. The paths of the two young men began to diverge. While Walpole dined and danced, Gray walked round the galleries, listened to concerts, or made careful records of his learned observations. Walpole, casting a casual glance over his shoulder at these activities, felt a spasm of irritation. "By a considerable volume of charts and pyramids, which I saw at Florence, I thought it threatened a publication," he told Ashton tartly.

In the Spring they proceeded to Rome. The old Pope had just died, and both young men were excited to have the chance of being there when a new one was elected. Change of scene did nothing to bring them closer together. Walpole was bored by Rome. The historical sights were no doubt extraordinary enough to revive a little his waning interest in sightseeing; and he enjoyed bargaining for objets d'art, with a view to setting up as a collector. On the other hand, society

HORACE WALPOLE IN MASQUERADING DRESS
DURING HIS ITALIAN TOUR
From a portrait by Rosalba Carriera in the possession of the Lord Walpole

was stuffy and dull, the Pope did not get elected, there was no Carnival, and no Mann. Taking it all in all, Florence was much more agreeable. He solaced himself by writing frequent letters to Mann about the goings-on of the Old Pretender, who was now visiting Rome.

Gray, too, was interested to see so celebrated a personage.

"I have more time than I thought, and I will employ it in telling you about a Ball that we were at the other evening. Figure to yourself a Roman villa; all its little apartments thrown open, and lighted up to the best advantage. At the upper end of the gallery, a fine concert, in which La Diamantina, a famous virtuosa, played on the violin divinely, and sung angelically; Giovannino and Pasqualini (great names in musical story) also performed miraculously. On each side were ranged all the secular grand monde of Rome, the Ambassadors, Princesses, and all that. Among the rest Il Serenissimo Pretendente (as the Mantove Gazette calls him) displayed his rueful length of person, with his two young ones, and all his ministry around him. 'Poi nacque un grazioso ballo', where the world danced, and I sat in a corner regaling myself with iced fruits, and other rinfrescatives."

This letter tells us something about Gray, as well as about the Old Pretender. Even when he was persuaded to go to a ball, he did not dance, but sat in a corner. There is an acid undertone to the urbane sentences in which he relates these facts. Indeed, he was beginning to feel the limitations of his position unpleasantly; and in more ways than one. Why was he too poor to be able to buy antiques easily? He knew he appreciated them more than many who could. All the same, unlike Walpole, Gray was not disappointed in Rome. Not a step he took, but he set his foot upon some reverent history.

There was the Colosseum, there was the Forum, there was Frascati to visit, Palestrina, the myriad rainbow-tinted cascades of Tivoli, Alba with its memories of Pompey's villa; there were the tombs and broken aqueducts of the Appian Way. No doubt, as Walpole told him, these places, apart from their historic associations, were no better worth seeing than Richmond or Windsor. But such associations were to one with Gray's intensity of historical imagination, the source of half his pleasures in seeing anything.

"I am now at home," he breaks out to West, "and going to the window to tell you it is the most beautiful of Italian nights, which, in truth, are but just begun. . . . There is a moon! there are stars for you! Do not you hear the fountain? Do not you smell the orange flowers? That building yonder is the Convent of S. Isidore; and that eminence, with the cypress trees and pines upon it, the top of M. Quirinal. This is all true, and yet my prospect is not 200 yards in length."

For two months, broken by an excursion to Naples, they lingered on in Rome, waiting in vain for the Cardinals to come to a decision about the election. At last, Walpole's impatience got the better of him. He decided to go back to Florence. Gray could willingly have stayed for months more, happily spelling out time-blurred inscriptions, and conjuring up gorgeous visions of imperial Rome from crumbling arch and grass-grown foundation. But since Walpole paid the piper, he must call the tune. Protestingly, Gray submitted.

Back at Florence, their life took up its old course. But the divergence between the friends was now more open. It is to be noted that they no longer lived under the same roof: Walpole stayed with Mann, Gray had rooms in a neighbouring house. In spirit, they were yet more widely separated. Wal-

pole enjoyed Florence more than ever. He loved the lounging,
festive way of life; getting up at twelve, dining at three, and
then a succession of strolls and little parties, that ended with a
late supper of iced fruit out of doors on the marble bridge,
with the violins discoursing delicate music to the stars.
Florentine society, too, now struck him as the most agreeable
in the world, as it loitered through the radiant summer days,
gaily gossiping, lightly making love. For no longer did
Walpole look with contempt on the ceremonious philander-
ings of lady and Cicisbeo. On the contrary, he aspired to be
a Cicisbeo himself; embarked on a cool elegant amour with
the beautiful Countess Grifone. Mann, too, was as good company as ever, and Walpole met with a new friend in the
person of a Mr. Chute, who, with his cousin, Whithed, was
travelling in Italy. Cultured and entertaining, Chute would
lean back at the supper table, gesturing extravagantly with a
fan, to the disgust of more conventional Englishmen. Here
was another kindred spirit. Altogether, Walpole had never
felt happier.

Not so Gray. He did, it is true, very much like Chute,
who in addition to his other charms, turned out to be
very musical, and so concerned about his health that he lived
almost entirely on milk and turnips. Gray also appreciated
the sensuous pleasures of life in Florence, the beauty of the
town, the fruit and ices, and above all, the wonderful Italian
weather, so warm that he could sit on his balcony late into
the night, clad only in his dressing gown, watching the
waters of the Arno, as they lapsed by, gleaming inky in the
brilliant moonlight. But he was not happy. "Florence," he
said, "is an excellent place to employ all one's animal senses
in, but utterly contrary to one's rational powers." Something
fundamental in his nature, something bourgeois, English,
Protestant, rose up in outraged affront, against the glittering
conscienceless hedonism of the South. He sought to occupy

himself by making a collection of music, and by writing a long Latin poem about the philosophy of Locke. Even this desperate remedy, however, did not stop him from feeling that he was wasting his time.

Dissatisfaction with his mode of life was sharpened by a growing exasperation with Walpole, an exasperation in which personal resentment was swelled by moral disapproval. Surely it was shocking that a man of Walpole's intelligence should throw away his opportunities for improving the mind for the sake of such vapid frivolities. One instance of this seems particularly to have rankled with Gray. There were several places of interest in the neighbourhood that they had missed seeing on their first visit. Gray wanted to visit them now. Walpole, however, after Rome and Naples, was finally sick of sightseeing. He said he would not go, though he offered to send Gray without him. At this, to him, insulting proposal, Gray's temper began to give way. He told Walpole what he thought of his selfishness and triviality. Peppery Walpole was not the man to stand this; and from Gray, of all people. Who was he to lecture him? Sharply he would remind Gray of his dependent position. Gray, deeply hurt, rushed off to Mann, to whom he poured out in floods of tears his despair at Walpole's apparent change of feeling towards him. With Mann's tactful help, the quarrel would be smoothed over; but only temporarily. Another rub brought another row. Clearly things could not go on like this. Indeed the crisis in their relationship was approaching. It is now that we feel most acutely our want of sufficient information about the story. There is not a word in the letters left to us to trace exactly the steps that lead to the final breach. All we know is that the storm finally broke in August at the little town of Reggio, where they had gone to see the Fair. Its immediate occasion seems to have been some trouble about a letter written by Gray to Ashton. Perhaps Walpole opened it, and

found some disagreeable remarks about himself. Perhaps—
and this is more likely—Ashton, thinking he could ingratiate
himself with Walpole by a little discreet mischief-making,
repeated Gray's words in a letter to Walpole. Anyway
Walpole taxed Gray with treachery, and a furious quarrel
blazed up, which ended with Gray leaving immediately and
dramatically for Venice. A few days later, Walpole, seized
with a fit of remorse, asked Gray to come back for a reconciliation. Gray came, but only to declare himself adamant.
It was six years before they spoke to one another again.

Such was the celebrated quarrel between Gray and Walpole. Many years later Walpole wrote an account of it, in
which he took most of the blame for it on himself.

"I am conscious that in the beginning of the differences
between Gray and me, the fault was mine. I was too young,
too fond of my own diversions, nay I do not doubt, too
much intoxicated by indulgence, vanity, and the insolence
of my situation as a Prime Minister's son, not to have been
inattentive and insensible to the feelings of one I thought
below me; of one whom presumption and folly perhaps
made me deem not my superior *then* in parts, though I
have since felt my infinite inferiority to him. I treated him
insolently: he loved me and I did not think he did."

This is very handsome of him: it seems hard that most
subsequent writers on the subject have taken him at his word,
and speak as though Gray was the injured party. As a matter
of fact, from the scanty information we have, he seems to
have behaved the more unreasonably of the two. After all,
it was natural for a young man of twenty-one like Walpole
to want to dance and flirt: Gray was the odd one to prefer
inspecting ancient monuments. Moreover, Walpole could
not be expected to plan his tour just to suit Gray's tastes. Nor,

though he sometimes felt irritated with him, did he try and divert Gray from them. He was perfectly willing to live and let live. Besides he showed the more generous feelings on the matter. Did not he in the end apologize and try to make it up? But, if Gray were the more difficult, he was also far the most to be pitied. For he was the one who suffered: he it was who felt lonely and left out and awkward and poor. Above all, he was the one who cared the most. There is a crucial, revealing sentence in Walpole's statement. "He loved me, and I did not think he did." No doubt Walpole did not think so, because Gray had grown so disagreeable. In situations of this kind, the one who feels least is likely to make this mistake. Temperate affections are sufficiently under their owner's control for him to remember to try always be pleasant. Walpole's affection, for all its demonstrativeness, was of the temperate kind. He had too much to make him enjoy life to be dependent for his happiness on his relationship with any one person. This was not true of Gray. His disagreeableness was a proof of the peculiar and painful intensity of his attachment. He had very few friends; and his relationship to them was one of the few things that made life bright to him. Walpole was one of them. Gray had thought that his love for him was returned with equal strength. Gradually, inexorably, painfully, his experiences abroad had forced him to recognize that this was not so. This was why he could not resign himself to neglect; this was why it was unbearable for him to watch Walpole gossiping and flirting with Madame Grifone, when he could have gone away alone with him; this was why, finally, he could not bring himself to forgive him. Their situation in regard to one another was so delicate that they were bound to quarrel some time or other during the journey. But it was the fact that Gray was bitterly disillusioned in the tenderest depths of his heart that made the breach, when it did come, so catastrophic.

He lingered for a time at Venice, wretchedly depressed, and so hard up that he did not know how he could manage to pay for the journey home. Walpole, arriving at Venice a little later with Chute, was horrified to hear of his financial embarrassment. He did not dare, for fear of offending him, to offer him money directly, but contrived to get some to him disguised as a loan from Chute. In July Gray started to wend his sad way homewards. By September, 1741, he was in England.

Two days after his arrival he wrote to Chute.

"If this be London, Lord send me to Constantinople. Either I, or it, are extremely odd. The boys laugh at the depth of my ruffles, the immensity of my bagg, and the length of my sword. I am as an alien in my native land. Yea! I am as an owl among the small birds. It rains; everybody is discontented, and so am I. You cannot imagine how mortifying it is to fall into the hands of an English barber. . . . The natives are alive and flourishing. The fashion is a grey frock with round sleeves, bob-wig, or a spencer, plain hat with enormous brims and shallow crown, cock'd as bluff as possible; muslin neckcloth twisted round, rumpled, and tuck'd into the breast; all this with a certain seafaring air, as if they were just come back from Cartagena. If their pockets had anything in them, I should be afraid of everybody I met. Look in their face, they knock you down; speak to them, they bite off your nose. I am no longer ashamed in publick, but extremely afraid. If ever they catch me among 'em, I give them leave to eat me."

Indeed he had every reason to feel strange. It was not only his clothes that made him different from the unsettled inexperienced youth who had quitted England two years

before. He had come back a man; the same man, broadly
speaking, as he was to remain for the rest of his life. Let us
take a look at him. He is not so handsome as most famous
poets. A short plumpish figure with a tottery walk is surmounted by a head in which the noble impression made by a
lofty forehead and large dark eyes, eloquent beneath their
sharply pencilled angular brows, is contradicted by the tight
mouth and long prim chin. It is a sensitive, intellectual face;
it is also a stiff suspicious shut face. His demeanour was in
keeping with it. Shyness and awkwardness had taught themselves to hide behind an assumed air of disdain and an effemin-
ate affectedness of manner, which increased in proportion
as he felt that the people he was with did not like him. As for
the man beneath the manner, let Gray speak for himself.
There is a letter written to West during his last days at Florence, in which he gives an account of the changes he had
observed in his own character since he left England.

"As I am recommending myself to your love, methinks I
ought to send you my picture (for I am no more what I was,
some circumstances excepted, which I hope I need not
particularize to you); you must add then, to your former
ideas, two years of age, reasonable quantity of dullness, a
great deal of silence, and something that rather resembles,
than is, thinking; a confused notion of many strange and
fine things, that have swum before my eyes for some time,
a want of love for general society, indeed an inability to it.
On the good side you may add a sensibility for what others
feel, and indulgence for their faults or weaknesses, a love
of truth, and disdain of everything else. Then you are to
deduct a little impertinence, a little laughter, a good deal
of pride, and some spirits. These are all the alterations I
know of, you perhaps may find more. Think not that I
have been obliged, for this reformation of manners to

reason or reflection, but to a severer schoolmistress, Experience. One has little merit in learning her lessons, for one cannot well help it; but they are more useful than others, and imprint themselves in the very heart."

Gray was comically wrong in thinking that he was indulgent to the weaknesses of others. Walpole would have had something to tell West about this. But otherwise the account is fair enough. Gray's maturity appears in the detached clear-sightedness with which he could observe his own character. It was true that he was a sadder man; at least more consistently sad. Such remnants of boyish high spirits as had remained with him up to his departure, were now completely vanished. Experience had finally convinced him that his early suspicions of the world were justified. It was a hard disillusioning place, where happiness was transient, and sorrow sure; where few people shared his tastes or understood his feelings; and where no-one's affection seemed wholly to be trusted. "I am a fool to be surprised at meeting with brutishness or want of thought among mankind," he exclaimed bitterly. Moreover, he realized that he was peculiarly unfitted to battle with such a world. As he saw it, humanity was divided on the one hand into public sociable characters, whose nature and function it was to keep the world going, and on the other into private contemplative persons who must, if their natures were to find fulfilment, retire into their own inner life. He faced the fact that he belonged, for good or ill, irretrievably to the second category. He was at once too jealous of his own independence, and too bad at mixing with his fellows to hope for success in the mêlée. But even as a private person, he doubted if he was likely to be happy. Human life, of its nature, involved more pain than pleasure.

Yet he was not a pessimist in the full sense of the word. For one thing, the whole tradition of thought in which he had been brought up, would not let him be. Theoretically he believed in free will, in man's power to control his circumstances. "Our inclinations," he said, "are more than we imagine in our power; reason and resolution can direct them, and support us under many difficulties." Reason and resolution taught him that he must strive not to despair. Profoundly moral in his outlook he thought that man lived to be virtuous. And he did not doubt that suffering, if taken in the right spirit, so far from being an unmixed evil, was an aid to virtue. Did it not discipline the character and soften the heart to sympathize with the sufferings of others?

Gray was the more disposed to think this because he was a religious man. It was a sober straightforward Anglican sort of religion. He did not have mystical visions; and his mind was too unmetaphysical to appreciate the significance of dogmatic theology. But his poetical temperament, responsive as it was to the appeal of the ancient and the mysterious, made him unsympathetic to purely rationalist interpretations of the universe, and also susceptible to the religious sentiment. He readily accepted the creed in which he was brought up; and his faith in it was confirmed by that awe-inspiring sense of divinity that came to him at such times as his journey up to the Grande Chartreuse. Nor was his belief shaken by his melancholy. On the contrary, melancholy made him cling to it. Was not religion the only sure gleam of hope in a dark and disillusioning universe? Thinkers like Shaftesbury and Voltaire, who sought to undermine their fellow men's belief in it, were behaving to them with heartless and irresponsible cruelty. And Gray hated them for it.

The pleadings of piety and principle were further reinforced by those of good sense. Since life had to be lived, it was surely foolish not to make the best of it, rather than to waste one's time in unavailing lamentations against the Universal Plan. Besides, he must remember that he was not worse off than many other people, nor so admirable as to be justified in thinking he deserved to be specially saved from trouble. For all his pride, Gray was not self-pitying, nor unreasonably self-admiring. Even when, with an ironical eye, he watched his fellows absorbed in the world of business and pleasure without, apparently, a thought of the brevity and insignificance of their lives, he would remind himself that his own mode of living was not much superior—especially as he, unlike them, was not enjoying himself:

> "Methinks I hear in accents low," he sang,
> "The sportive kind reply:
> Poor moralist! And what art thou?
> A solitary fly!
> Thy joys no glittering female meets,
> No hive hast thou and hoarded sweets,
> No painted plumage to display:
> On hasty wings, thy youth is flown;
> Thy sun is set, thy Spring is gone—
> We frolic, while 'tis May."

He was the more easily able to take a balanced view of his lot, because there were things about it that he did enjoy. Its comic side for example; the spectacle of the world was entertaining as well as saddening. He could not look at it for long without finding something that forced him to smile. His cool, sharp-eyed sense of comedy was always glinting out to maintain his sense of proportion and impose a check upon his impulses of gloom. More important, the outer world was far from being the only world for Gray. Equally vivid was the world of his solitary imaginative life. And this had been enriched a thousand-fold by his years abroad. When he was by himself—reading, listening to music, gazing at mountains or ruined abbeys—his spirit suffered no sense of frustration; but expanded in a delight, which if not exactly ecstatic, was, within its sphere, endlessly satisfying. Nor was it merely a passive delight. What he read, what he heard, what he saw, stimulated him to think and analyse, dream and compose. This solitary Gray was very unlike the Gray whom the world knew. Gone were the nervous inhibitions, the prim regard for decorum. Instead, absorbed in an inner dream and for once utterly careless of outward appearances, he would loiter along, smiling, frowning, murmuring aloud to himself, and then suddenly flinging down, to lie for hours beneath the shadow of oak or beech tree. He was able to be so unselfconscious because he was at last on ground where he was confident. In the world of the imagination he knew he was not an alien. Spenser and Virgil would not let him down as his flesh and blood friends did. He did not feel out of it in ancient Rome as he did in modern Florence.

Thus, what with one thing and another, Gray strove to keep his tendency to melancholy within bounds. And for much of the time he succeeded in doing so.

"Mine, you are to know," he told West, "is a white melancholy, or rather Leucocholy for the most part; which though it seldom laughs or dances, nor even means what one calls Joy or Cheer, yet is a good easy sort of state, ça ne laisse que de s'amuser. The only fault of it is insipidity; which is apt now and then to give a sort of ennui, which makes one form certain little wishes that signify nothing. But there is another sorrow, black indeed, which I have now and then felt, that has somewhat in it like Tertullian's rule of faith, credo quia impossibile est; for it believes, nay, is sure of everything that is unlikely, so it be but frightful; and, on the other hand, excludes and shuts its eyes to the most possible hopes, and everything that is pleasurable; from this the Lord deliver us! For none but He and sunshiny weather can do it."

In this passage Gray was making things out a little better than they really were. In reality he did suffer from the black sort of melancholy more often than he wanted his correspondent to think. He admitted ruefully he found it easier to preach his gospel of good sense than to practise it. Indeed, he had special reason to be depressed at this time. Two things made life worth living to him, the life of contemplation and the love of his two intimate friends. He had quarrelled with one of these two; and was not able to feel any certainty of achieving the contemplative life. Practical and financial circumstances seemed likely to make it impossible. Nor was he the sort of man to alter such circumstances in the face of difficulty. Like many intellectual persons, Gray had remained immature in practical affairs, in proportion as he had matured mentally. Man has only a certain capacity for growth within him. All Gray's had gone into the development of his mind and heart: when it came to action he was still an inexperienced boy.

"Is it not odd," he writes to West; "to consider one's contemporaries in the grave light of husband and father? There is my Lords Sandwich and Halifax, they are statesmen: do not you remember them, dirty boys playing at cricket? As for me, I am never a bit the older, the bigger, nor the wiser than I was then." No—the problem of coping with the future was too difficult. Instead, turning his back on the world, he buried himself in reading or writing long letters on literary subjects to West. "You see by what I send you," he told him, "that I converse as usual with none but the dead: they are my old friends and almost make me long to be with them."

West responded to Gray as eagerly as ever. For, as much as ever, he needed him. During the two years his friends had been away, his life had grown steadily more unhappy. He had tried the Bar: but he disliked it so much that he had given it up. This brought him up against the same problem as

Gray. What was he to do instead? Vaguely and desperately he canvassed the various professions. First he thought of being a clergyman, then a soldier. This last was a preposterous idea: no one was less military. But the romantic-minded West was without much sense of reality. In the Army, he suddenly fancied, he might find means to cut the knot that held his life frustrated: either he would win glorious distinction or meet heroic death. Attracted by these alluring alternatives, he wrote off to Walpole, begging him to use his influence to get him a commission. Luckily Walpole, or the army authorities, showed a stronger grasp of fact than West: the letter produced no result. Anyway, by the time Gray got back to England any such active profession would have been out of the question for West. His always delicate health was breaking up. Moments of febrile agitation alternated with fits of lassitude in which he felt he could take no interest in anything: he was afflicted with a hacking cough which grew ominously worse with every month that passed. Whether West realized it or not, here were the dreadful symtoms of consumption. And now, if rumour is to be believed, mental anguish added itself to physical, to increase the strain on his already wasted frame. Dark hints reach us of a sinister drama of crime and guilty passion in which he was involved. He discovered unexpectedly, so it is said, that his mother, whom he loved and revered, was engaged in a sordid amour with an old friend of his own. It was even suggested that the two had conspired together to murder West's father in order that they might be able to marry each other. Whatever the truth of this lurid Hamlet-like tale, it is certain that in the Spring of 1742 West's condition took a quick turn for the worse. On 17th June Gray opened the newspaper and read some commemorative verses revealing the fact that West was dead.

The immediate shock was great; he had not realized how

ill his friend had been. The fundamental shock was greater. Even twenty years later, it was noticed that he could not mention West's death without nearly breaking down. Indeed it had produced the central crisis of his life. For, coming as the culmination of a sombre year of calamity, it broke his last link with the steady solid happiness of Eton days. Experience had not hardened Gray's heart. On the contrary, disillusionment with mankind in general had made him cling all the more desperately to those few individuals with whom he could feel in sympathy. After the quarrel with Walpole, West was the only one of those left. On to him had flowed forth all the force of Gray's thwarted, powerful capacity for affection: on to West who was as shy and sensitive and poor as himself, who cared for books and meditation as much as he did, and whom, he knew, would never be seduced away from him by the tawdry glitter of the world. Now West was gone. How right he had been—more cruelly, horribly right even than he had imagined—in thinking life a cheat! Even if for once one did find a friend who could be trusted to be faithful, yet it was impossible to be sure of keeping him. The ruthless impersonal forces of disaster and death might wrest him away just when one needed him most. There was no end to life's capacity to wound poor helpless humanity.

The structure of philosophy and piety that he had carefully erected to shield him from the blows of fate, was exposed to the full blast of misfortune. It stood the strain. That it did so is evidence of the strength of mind that lurked within his frail, fussy body. Gray did not allow himself to fall into despair. What is more remarkable, he did not grow apathetic. On the contrary, the unprecedented turmoil of emotion which swelled up in his heart at this culminating disaster quickened his spirit to an unprecedented activity. Gray was born a creative artist: deep within him glinted a spark of the true divine fire. But it was not a strong spark: and somehow he had never yet managed to heat it up to an active flame. Constitutional languor had something to do with this. He was further inhibited by too highly developed a critical faculty. If he did screw himself up to begin writing something, he soon grew disgusted with the result, and dropped it. Now at last the pressure of anguish broke down his inhibitions. His heart was so full that he felt compelled to unburden it—and never mind if the result was not all he wished! For once his temperament was warmed to an intensity that had to find release in creation. It is not the first time that the suffering of the man has been the salvation of the artist.

As usually happens, his creative mood came upon him a little time after the experience which engendered it, when he was able to recollect his emotion in sufficient tranquillity to turn it into poetry. In August Gray went to Stoke Poges, near Eton, to stay with an aunt. There, as he roamed about the Buckinghamshire countryside lying placid in the summery stillness, all the confused surging flood of thought and feeling which had agitated him during the last few months began unbidden to settle and crystallize and take shape in phrase and stanza. Poem after poem streamed from his pen. They formed a considered comment on his whole previous history. In them appear all the dominating and characteristic phases of his sentiment: his passionate love for his friends, his responsiveness to the beauties of art and nature, his feeling for the ancient past, his sadness, his acute awareness of the vanity of human wishes. And along with them the forces, which he invoked to govern his emotions, also found expression; his stoicism, his piety, his irony. So that the sentiments that inspired them come to us subdued into a measured elegiac sadness, lit once or twice by a bitter-sweet smile. Now he asserts his determination to profit by the hard lessons of adversity: "Teach me to love and to forgive!" he cries—was he thinking of Walpole? Now gazing across the fields to where the russet towers of Eton loomed faintly through the hazy August distance, like the visible ghosts of his happy irretrievable past, he moralizes on the contrast between his present mood and that of the care-free days of boyhood.

> "Ah happy hills! Ah pleasing shade!
>   Ah fields beloved in vain!
> Where once my careless childhood strayed
>   A stranger yet to pain.
> I feel the gales that from ye blow
> A momentary bliss bestow,
> As waving fresh their gladsome wing,
> My weary soul they seem to soothe
> And, redolent of joy and youth,
> To breathe a second spring."

Now as the beloved figure of West rose before his mental eye, his grief sighed itself forth in quiet, beautiful, hopeless lamentation.

> "In vain to me the smileing Morning's shine,
>   And redning Phoebus lifts his golden Fire;
> The Birds in vain their amorous Descant joyn;
>   Or chearful Fields resume their green Attire;
> These Ears, alas! for other Notes repine,
>   A different Object do these Eyes require:
> My lonely Anguish melts no Heart but mine;
>   And in my Breast the imperfect Joys expire.
> Yet morning smiles the busy Race to chear,
>   And new-born Pleasure brings to happier Men:
> The Fields to all their wonted Tribute bear;
>   To warm their little Loves the Birds complain:
> I fruitless mourn to him that cannot hear,
>   And weep the more because I weep in vain."

One evening wandering in the rural churchyard of Stoke Poges, scattered with mossy time-blurred gravestones, hints of a grander conception began to shadow themselves forth in his imagination; it's theme, human life looked at in the light of its inevitable end. How transient it was! How insignificant its greatest men and most famous achievements! And for that matter, its most dreadful woes. To let oneself be overwhelmed by them was as futile as to be dazzled by its achievements.

> "The thoughtless World to Majesty may bow,
>   Exalt the brave and idolize Success;
> But more to Innocence their Safety owe
>   Than Power and Genius e'er conspir'd to bless.
>
> And thou, who mindful of th'unhonour'd Dead,
>   Dost in these Notes their artless Tale relate,
> By Night and lonely Contemplation led
>   To linger in the gloomy Walks of Fate:
>
> Hark! how the sacred Calm, that broods around,
>   Bids ev'ry fierce tumultuous Passion cease;
> In still small Accents whisp'ring from the Ground,
>   A grateful Earnest of eternal Peace.
>
> No more, with Reason and thyself at Strife,
>   Give anxious Cares and endless Wishes room;
> But thro' the cool sequester'd Vale of Life
>   Pursue the silent Tenour of thy Doom."

Thus, in sculptured phrase, and grave tolling music, spoke themselves forth the deepest conclusions borne in on Gray from twenty-six years of troubled life. But before he had time to organize them into a complete work, the wave of emotion which had borne him up since June began to ebb: and with it the creative energy which was its expression. Languor and self-criticism once more began to assert their inhibiting hand. His aesthetic impulse spent itself, never to return with the same strength. But it had lasted long enough to place him among the great English poets. The most miserable year of his life turned out also to be the most fruitful.

It also decided him finally to take up a life of retirement. Bruised by grief, his spirit now shrank uncontrollably from the hurly-burly of the rough world. His one sortie into it had turned out too painful for him to consider risking another. He did not like to declare this openly, for his mother, ambitious for his future, still wanted him to go to the Bar. But he got round this difficulty by telling her that he could read Law just as well at Cambridge. For it was Cambridge Gray now chose as his refuge. Not that his feeling had changed about the place. He still thought it odiously uncouth and provincial. But practical reasons made it the only choice. By the easygoing University regulations of those days he could go on residing in the college free, for as long as he wanted. Accordingly in October, 1742, we find him unpacking his boxes in Peterhouse once more. In accents of half-bitter, half-humorous resignation, he greeted his unrevered Alma Mater.

"Hail, horrors, hail! ye ever gloomy bowers,
    Ye gothic fanes, and antiquated towers,
    Where rushy Camus' slowly-winding flood
    Perpetual draws his humid train of mud:
    Glad I revisit thy neglected reign,
    Oh take me to thy peaceful shade again."

III

We know nothing about Gray for the next two years. Presumably, shut away from the world in the brown and healing silence of library and college room, he set to work to mend his heart and re-establish his equilibrium. If so, he was successful. When he re-emerges, he is his urbane composed self once more. His spirits have stabilized: so has his mode of life. Human beings can be divided into those who allow themselves to be the sport of circumstances, those who try and force circumstances to their will, and those who, while accepting circumstances in the main, in detail seek to manipulate them to suit their desires. Of this last category, Gray is an outstanding example. All he had gone through during his first twenty-six years had left him with a clear idea of what he wanted to have in life, and also of what he was likely to get. For he was far too sensible to fancy he could get all he wanted. Accordingly, cautious and unhurried, he proceeded to devise a plan of living, the best for his taste and temperament possible in the conditions in which fate had seen fit to place him. Having established it, he stuck to it. Though in later years he sometimes got a chance of making a change, he always refused it at once. No doubt his plan of life had its disadvantages. But so, also, as far as he could see, had every other plan. Why then change? Further, he had matured so early that his inner self was no longer susceptible of much development. He and his form of life are alike fixed. The consequence is that after his return to Cambridge his story, as a story, almost comes to an end. Reading it is less like following a stream than contemplating a pool.

It is, however, a pool well worth contemplating; as it lies secluded in its green shade and with a whole soft landscape of lawn and sky and antique spire reflected in its calm surface. Its setting was Cambridge. Gray desired a life of retirement and study in which he would not have to suffer the humiliation of being dependent on anyone else. At Cambridge, he had all the books and quiet he wanted: and he could live there in independence. Not an easy independence. Gray was still very poor: this was one of the inevitable disadvantages forced on him by circumstances. Sometimes he found himself compelled to borrow forty guineas from a friend in order to keep going. He could imagine too vividly the pleasures of affluence—going where he felt inclined, buying all the pretty things he wanted, and seeing as much as he liked of those few persons with whom he did feel an affinity—not to mind poverty. "It is a foolish thing," he sighed, "that one can't, not only not live as one pleases, but where and with whom one pleases, without money. Swift somewhere says that money is liberty: and I fear money is friendship too, and society, and almost every external blessing. It is a great, though ill-natured comfort to see most of those who have it in plenty, without pleasure, without liberty, and without friends."

It was no use repining though. He had better make up his mind that his Peterhouse rooms were his permanent home: and to make them as agreeable as conditions permitted. This cannot have been difficult. The low-ceilinged, sash-windowed set of apartments, set high in the fourth floor above the peaceful small-town busyness of King's Parade, made a pleasant place of retirement. Gray saw that the college servant kept them meticulously clean and tidy: and gradually accumulated in them such amenities as his exiguous purse could command. There were his books and prints and collection of music, there was his little pianoforte, there were a handsome pair of blue and white Japanese vases—these were a great feature of his domestic interior—above all there were flowers. Mignonette bloomed in the windows, bright nosegays were placed about the room: so that with the smell of leather and old woodwork, was blended ever a fresh waft of garden sweetness.

So much for the physical framework of his days. The mental was provided by his scheme of work. "Employment is happiness" was one of his favourite maxims: and he was always occupied in a definite course of study. From time to time the subject of this altered. During the first years his main interests seem to have been classical; Plato, the Greek Anthology, Strabo. He meditated an edition of Strabo at one time. Later his curiosity turned to English poetry, more especially its obscure origins in Provençal song, Anglo-Saxon epic and the Norse sagas. How interesting to write a history of it! He got as far as making a rough plan for such a work. Before he had got far with it, however, he became interested in Gothic architecture, then almost virgin soil in England. In the last years of his life Gothic in its turn was supplanted by natural science, above all that branch of natural science, botany, which he had loved ever since he went gathering bog asphodel in the fields round Eton. Gray's curiosity was boundless, and his standard of knowledge rigidly high. Here was where his academic training had left its mark on him. He did not feel justified in coming to any conclusion till he had taken trouble to learn everything that could possibly be thought relevant to the subject. Each successive interest involved him in exploring fields far outside his original intention. Thus English poetry led him to learn Icelandic; Gothic architecture proved unintelligible without a thorough knowledge of heraldry and mediaeval history. Archaeology, zoology, philology—he had gone into them all before he had finished. It is not surprising to learn that he ended up as one of the most learned men in Europe. Nor, though his knowledge was so diverse, was it disordered. In the library at Cambridge one can still see the notebooks in which, logically ordered and neatly written, lie the lucid record of his researches. He also found time to keep a naturalist's calendar in which each day he noted down such things as the temperature, the prevailing wind, what flowers were coming into bud, what birds were singing. For example:

1760. April 20.
      Therm. at 60. Wind S.W. Chaffinch, lark, thrush, wren and robin singing. Horse chestnut, wild briar, Bramble, and Sallow had spread their leaves. Hawthorn and Lilac had formed their blossoms. Blackthorn, double Peach, Peas in full bloom. Double Jonquils, Hyacinths, Anemones, single Wallflowers, and Auriculas in flower. In the fields Dog violets, Daisies, Dandelion, Buttercups, Red-Archangel and Shepherd's purse.

Such an entry, where a poet's sensibility glints involuntarily through the sober factual botanist's phrasing is curiously characteristic of Gray's tone of mind.

Serious study did not occupy all his time. Gray had not the vitality for continuous work: and much of his day was given up to rest and pleasure. His pleasures were as deliberately pursued as his work. They were mainly aesthetic. Music was a chief one. The silence of his room was often broken by the frail sound of the pianoforte, as he sat playing Scarlatti and Vivaldi: Italian music was his favourite. Gray could sing too; without much voice, but—so the few friends, whom he allowed to hear him, said—with a sensitive understanding of the music. He also sketched, walked, took an interest in landscape gardening, interior decoration, dress and cookery. Into these activities he carried the methodical habits of his serious studies. There is indeed something slightly comic in his passion for making lists and classifications. It seemed as if he was ready to catalogue anything. Even the blank pages of his cookery book are filled with lists of pots and pans and ingredients, receipts, arranged "in a scientific order", and accurately indexed to their respective pages. If a friend asked his advice about decorating his house, back would come a lengthy disquisition on wallpaper and window glass, complete with sizes of patterns and lists of prices. "I much doubt of the effect colours—any others than the tints of stucco—would have on a Gothic design on paper. Those I saw at Ely were green and pale blue with the raised work white, if you care to hazard it. One of threepence a yard in small compartments thus might perhaps do for the stairs."

He did not stay at Cambridge all the time. Once or twice a year, after diligent consideration, he would go off for a change. Sometimes it was a brief change, just a day or two in London to listen to a concert or an opera. In Summer his excursions were more extended. For some years he spent August and September at Stoke Poges. His father had died soon after Gray got back to England: and his mother had retired to settle with her sister at Stoke. Gray's affection for her would have made him feel he ought to spend part of the year with her in any circumstances. It cannot have been a disagreeable obligation though: he was the sort of man who feels easy in the society of old ladies, and he loved the country. In 1753, however, his mother died, her sister four years later. Gray took to spending his summer holidays in stately solitary little pilgrimages to some place famous for natural beauty or artistic and historical interest—cathedrals, ruined castles, Elizabethan mansions, the coast of Sussex, the Lake country. He got as far as Scotland once. Each journey led to a new spate of closely-packed, neatly-written notebooks.

In the intervals of sight-seeing, he also visited his friends; Wharton in Durham, Chute in Hampshire, Walpole at Strawberry Hill. For in the end he had made it up with

Walpole—or rather Walpole had made it up with him.
Walpole had never wanted to go on with the quarrel. And
when, in the Autumn of 1745, he heard from a mutual friend
that Gray was in a more approachable frame of mind, he wrote
off asking him to come and see him. Gray felt dubious. Such
an interview seemed likely to be very embarrassing: and
besides he was not at all sure he wanted a reconciliation. He
was not one who forgot a quarrel easily, especially when he
felt he had been wholly in the right about it. However,
good sense and curiosity between them triumphed over his
hesitations: so one evening in November he paid a call on
Walpole at his house in Arlington Street. The meeting did
not go off very well, at least as far as Gray was concerned.
Once more the differences between the two men entertain-
ingly reveal themselves. Gray's moralistic outlook and his
romantic conception of the higher friendship alike led him to
think that personal relations should be conducted on a basis
of absolute frankness and sincerity. Unless he could be given
a thorough and satisfying explanation of Walpole's behaviour
to him in Italy, he did not feel justified in forgiving and
forgetting. It is doubtful whether he was right about this.
Thorough explanations generally involve home truths: and
home truths seldom produce good will. Anyway, Walpole
had no intention of embarking on anything of the kind. He
always hated going into things. Besides, accustomed as he
was to the thousand ephemeral insignificant tiffs of the
fashionable world, and skilled in all its graceful white lies and
easy breezy evasions, he saw no necessity for explanations.
Far better to behave as if nothing had happened. Accordingly
when Gray, stiff with shyness and suspicion, entered the room,
Walpole rushed towards him, kissed him warmly on both
cheeks—"with all the ease of one who receives an acquaintance just out of the country"—and, pressing him into a
fauteuil, poured out for three hours an uninterrupted torrent

of Beau Monde gossip. "I took my leave very indifferently pleased, but treated with wondrous good-breeding," said Gray sarcastically. However he was not so put off as to refuse Walpole's invitation to dine the next day. This went better: a third interview on the following morning, in which Gray did manage to extract some sort of explanation of his previous conduct from Walpole—as much, he thought, as he was ever likely to get—confirmed his favourable impression.

He was the more willing to receive it because, during his stay in London, he had become convinced that the person most to blame in his quarrel with Walpole had been Ashton. Ashton had been dining with Walpole the same night as Gray. Taking the line that he had more reason to complain of Gray than Gray of him, he had insisted on coming to see him the next morning to explain his part in the whole affair. The interview should have made Gray realize the dangers attendant on frank explanations. The more Ashton explained, the worse did his conduct appear. There was no question that here was the end of this friendship. In his subsequent correspondence, Gray only refers to Ashton once at any length: and that is as a character in a nightmare.

Meanwhile, during the next months, Walpole continued his advances. Gray was still a trifle suspicious. "There has been *in appearance*," he said, "the same kindness and confidence almost as of old: what is the motive I cannot yet guess." Gradually, however, he began to thaw. By the time two years had passed, a relationship had re-established itself between them that was to endure for life.

It was not the same sort of relationship that it once had been. Each knew too much about the other for that to be possible: Gray in particular was never going to forget how badly, in his opinion, Walpole was capable of behaving. And both, if irritated, could say very acid things about each other. The romantic friendship of youth, founded on a rapturous sense of soul affinity, was over for good and all. In its place was a middle-aged friendship based on a rational community of tastes. It was a more stable basis, especially since Walpole, with the advancing years, became less predominantly interested in social life as compared with art and letters. More and more he grew to value someone with whom he could talk of book-bindings and painted glass, of Anne Boleyn's ruff and the Duke of Bedford's genealogy. For this purpose who so good as Gray? Walpole had only to hazard a query on one of those topics, and back would come six pages of minute, reliable information, complete, of course, with references. It was better still when Gray came to Strawberry Hill, and they could talk. Gray was very much at home at Strawberry Hill. He liked the company, he liked the stylishness, he liked the fantasy. Every time he came, there was something new to admire: a ceiling powdered with papier maché stars, a chimney piece inspired by the High Altar of Rouen Cathedral, a bed hung with purple cut velvet on a ground of stone-coloured satin. A decorous Georgian gentleman, Gray wandered through the "long-drawn aisles and fretted vaults" of the queer miniature mock-Gothic dream palace, with feelings of great satisfaction. Nor, though he might shrink from himself taking part in the life of the great world, was he so changed as no longer to like hearing about it at secondhand. The whiff of high fashion and high politics he got from Walpole's conversation still had power mildly to intoxicate him. And he still laughed at Walpole's jokes. So did Walpole at his. Perhaps this was the strongest bond between them. A common taste in humour, the inclination to find the same things comically incongruous, reveals the deepest kind of affinity of spirit: deeper far than that implied by a common creed or cause. Once, by way of cheering up the grief-stricken Lady Waldegrave, the two read aloud to her the autobiography of the seventeenth century Lord Herbert of Cherbury. "We could not get on for laughing and screaming," says Walpole. No wonder he found Gray such a kindred spirit. There can have been few people in England who found Lord Herbert a side-splitting author.

Unexpectedly Walpole turned out to be practically useful to Gray: and in a very important way. Once relations were resumed between them, Gray fell back into his old habit of sending Walpole anything he had written, for criticism. He showed him the group of poems he had composed after West's death: and also newer efforts, including, bit by bit as it slowly grew to completion, the Elegy in the Country Churchyard. Walpole—it was one of his attractive qualities —could admire passionately, especially the work of a friend. Gray's poems gave him something worth admiring. He bubbled over with excitement. Here surely was true genius! He showed the poems round in manuscript; and later persuaded Gray to let him get them published—all the more ardently because he fancied himself as an impresario and much enjoyed busily supervising the details of printing and publication. It was lucky he did; for Gray turned out to be extremely difficult in these matters. Not only was he endlessly fussy about the form in which his work appeared, but he was so suspicious that he was liable to fancy that Walpole and the publisher were deliberately conspiring together to defeat his wishes. The most trivial points—the size in which his name was printed on the title-page, a proposal that his portrait should be used as a frontispiece—was enough to produce a violent explosion of prima donna temperament. To meet it Walpole brought all his diplomatic talents into play. He wrote back at once in answer to Gray's hysterical expostulations, sympathizing, explaining, cajoling, soothing. But it generally took two or three letters to get the agitated poet back into anything like a reasonable frame of mind.

It was ungrateful of Gray to be so difficult. For Walpole

was, in fact, making him famous. It was a slack time in English poetry. Nothing of the first interest by a new writer had appeared for several years. As the result the impression made by Gray's poems, and in particular by the Elegy, was tremendous. Statesmen and generals quoted it: Stoke Poges Churchyard became a celebrated place. Within a few years and on the strength of half a dozen shortish poems, Gray was acknowledged by almost everybody as the first of ving English poets.

Walpole was far from being his only great friend. Gray had always prized the pleasures of friendship as much as those of learning and art. And he made it part of his plan of life to cultivate them. If he chanced to come across a kindred spirit— it was not often—he set aside time to establish and maintain a relation with him. Every few years, a new name appears among his correspondents: gradually he accumulated a circle. Old friends formed its nucleus; Walpole, Chute, Brown, Wharton. Later, and more especially after Gray became famous, it was enlarged by the addition of some younger men who were drawn to him by his distinction and looked upon him as their master. These youthful friendships meant a great deal to Gray. They did something to fill the gap made in his emotional life by his celibacy. Gray had enough in common with young men, given they were of a sympathetic type, not to feel awkward with them, as he did with young women: nor was he bothered by the fear lest friendship with them might rouse sentimental expectations that he could not fulfil. Yet their ardour and high spirits and fresh young faces gave their company some of the gay exhilarating sweetness that less inhibited men find in that of girls. Through them also he was enabled to experience at second hand as it were and belatedly, a little of the youth he had never had. The young men with their boyish gusto and confidence and irresponsibility let in an invigorating breath of morning to the cloistered twilight of his prematurely middle-aged existence. In a discreet sort of way Gray unbent with his young disciples, liked teasing them, scolding them, talking nonsense with them. And instructing them: where we come to the third source of the peculiar charm he found in their society. He was a born don: the relation of master to pupil suited him. Having the advantage in age made him less shy, especially since—combined with his position—it interposed a respectful barrier between him and the risk of any impertinence on the pupil's part. With enthusiasm he threw himself into the task of opening a young man's mind, refining his taste, directing his studies, sympathizing with him in his difficulties, warning, advising. If one of his young friends sent him a poem he had written, Gray would put all his own work aside, to go through it line by line and send back an elaborate criticism. Indeed, Gray was master of the art of friendship between older and younger man. His disciples got all the benefit of his learning and stimulating intelligence, made soft and light by the glow of his affection. But he did not spoil and he did not flatter: while his rational sense of his position stopped him from ever letting the relationship become undignified and over-familiar.

Whether the young men were always worth the attention he lavished on them is another matter. The only two whose figures are at all clear to us, William Mason and Norton Nicholls, are of the type that had always attracted him: clever, precocious, vivacious youths, gossipy with an edge of malice to their gossip, and much given to sentiment and culture. Mason was in addition a poet. His letters are an odd mixture of spicy anecdotes about high life, and lengthy disquisitions on a ponderous tragedy he had written on the formidable subject of Caractacus. Gray smiled at the anecdotes and—strange to relate of one so critical—was much impressed by Caractacus. He was very fond of Mason, called him "Scrod-

dles", and twitted him playfully about his long nose. Norton
Nicholls he teased too—about his curious Christian name.
"How can people subscribe such a devil of a name—I warrant
you call it a Christian name—to their letters, as you do. I
always thought I had a small matter of aversion for you
mechanically rising in me, and doubtless this was the reason.
Fie, fie! put on a white satin mantle and be carried to church
again."

Otherwise—though Gray was careful to tell Nicholls how
little he thought intellectual accomplishments should be
valued in comparison with moral virtue—his discourse to
him was mainly about learned topics. These had brought
them together. They had met in 1761 drinking tea at another
don's rooms. Gray had quoted a line of Milton: Norton had
suggested that it was an echo of Dante. "Sir, do you read
Dante?" cried Gray, turning to him with excited interest.
From that instant they were close friends. Others might find
Nicholls an affected coxcomb; Gray saw nothing to complain
of in him. While Nicholls constituted himself the champion
of Gray against any breath of criticism. Fancy a frivolous
dilettante like Mr. Walpole presuming to quarrel with his
"dear Mr. Gray!" It only showed how unworthy he was to
be his friend. Nicholls' attitude to Gray—and Mason's too—
is a trifle irritating; the assiduity with which they play up to
him, the proprietary tone they assume when talking of him
to those inferior beings who have not been admitted to the
privilege of his intimacy. The professional disciple of the
great is a tiresome type. One is not surprised to learn that
both Mason and Nicholls turned later into successful men-of-
the-world clergymen.

Amid the all-male cast of Gray's circle appears one female
name. This was yet another result of his literary fame. In the
summer of 1750, Walpole had been showing the manuscript
of the Elegy round to such of his friends as went in for culture:

F   149

among them a certain Lady Cobham who, with her ward, the twenty-one-year-old Miss Henrietta Speed, lived at the Manor House of Stoke Poges. Both professed themselves in ecstasy at the poem. How thrilling to think that the author was sometimes a neighbour! They longed to know him. With Miss Speed to wish was to act. One afternoon, Gray, returning from his daily walk, was surprised to find a mysterious note on his writing table. "Lady Schaub's compliments to Mr. Gray," it ran, "she is sorry not to find him at home, to tell him that Lady Brown is very well." Lady Brown was a distant acquaintance of Gray's: Lady Schaub, a friend of her's, was staying with Lady Cobham. Miss Speed, discovering the tenuous link, had made use of it to scrape acquaintance. Politeness required that Gray should make a return call. He enjoyed it enormously. The old Elizabethan mansion, with its mullions and panelling and dark discursive passages and picturesque associations with Sir Christopher Hatton, was just the place to appeal to his imagination. Nor were its inhabitants less agreeable than their dwelling. Lady Cobham was pleasant: Miss Speed was more. Plump, dark and prepossessing-looking, she united the finished agreeability of a woman of fashion to a quick satirical intelligence and an irrepressible vitality that made her enjoy everything. Though not intellectual herself, she liked the society of intellectual men, and knew just how to make them like her. Now she devoted herself to drawing Gray out. It is unlikely that it had ever happened to him before. He succumbed at once. So inspired indeed was he by her company, that, on getting home, he sat down and wrote off a comic poem for her about the unusual circumstances of their meeting. Miss Speed replied enthusiastically appreciative, and with another invitation. Gray accepted. It led to other meetings. Soon his friends were amused to hear that Gray was spending his summer rattling about in a butcher's cart, driven by the spirited hands of Miss Speed.

This, as might be expected, was followed by a rumour that he was in love with her. Everything we know about Gray goes to make this unlikely. But, as much as most artists, he responded to the pleasure of being lionized by a lady of fashion, more especially as this particular lady, with her Walpole-like mixture of spirits, wit and modishness, was just the type to please him. Nor was he averse to a pretence of flirtation. Though he denied to his friends that he was in love, it was in a tone of gratified coyness, that indicated that he rather liked them to think he was. After all it was a new thing for him to be suspected of an entanglement with a fine lady. He even tried in a mild way to play up to his rôle in it. When Miss Speed told him she would like to hear his muse sing of love, he answered with a correct little copy of eighteenth century amorous verse addressed to her under the name of Delia.

"Sighs sudden and frequent, looks ever dejected,
    Sounds that steal from my tongue, by no meaning connected:
    Ah say, Fellow Swains, how these symptoms befell me?
    They smile, but reply not. Sure Delia will tell me."

Altogether the swooping down of this bright humming-bird into his quiet garden was pleasant enough for him to want to have it repeated. For the next few years it became a settled thing that during his stay at Stoke Poges, he should spend a good deal of time at the Manor House.

In addition to extending his inner circle, his renown brought him some pleasant acquaintances. Distinguished scholars and antiquarians entered into correspondence with him. Or a young nobleman would call at his rooms with a letter of introduction; Lord John Cavendish it might be, "a sensible boy, but awkward and bashful beyond belief and eats a buttock of beef at a meal"; or the magnificent Lord Nuneham. "You would delight in Lord Nuneham," Mason had written to him: "He's so peevish and hates things so much and has so much sense." Gray was certainly amused by him. Reeking of jessamine powder and arrayed in all the elaboration of great sleeves and a bouquet of jonquils—"a little too fine even for me, who love a little finery," said Gray—Lord Nuneham arrived in Cambridge at the time of the Newmarket races, only, it seemed, to advertise the fact that he did not think them worth attending. If it did not happen too often, Gray enjoyed a visit from a young nobleman. Talking to strangers was always an ordeal. But, if he had to entertain one, he preferred him to be polished, or at any rate, haloed by the romantic interest of a historic name.

Acquaintances, however, took up little of his time. It was not that he had lost interest in observing the world. He never tired of Walpole's social news; and his political too. A staunch Whig and a thorough-going patriot—what a wretched pack of fribbles the French were—Gray was all agog to hear the latest about the foundation of Pitt's government, or the progress of the Seven Years War. After the '45 rebellion he leapt at the chance of attending the trial of the Jacobite lords: observing, with sharp interested eye, how the tough old Balmerino casually fingered the edge of the axe that was to cut his head off. Equally he enjoyed the events of the Cambridge scene: Poor Smart the crazy poet has been arrested for debt, he gossips gaily to a correspondent; young Mr. Delaval has been sent down for having his mistress up to stay with him in College, disguised as an Army Captain; that old nuisance, Dr. Chapman of Magdalen has died from eating a whole turbot at one meal—"they say he made a very good end" commented Gray demurely. As from a box in a theatre, he sat gazing from the window of his rooms, at the comedy of University life.

But he did not go down on to the stage. There was little temptation. The dons were as stodgy as ever: and as for such female society as the place provided—"the women here," said he, "are few, squeezy and formal, and little skilled in amusing themselves or anyone else". Though, as a matter of fact, even if Cambridge society had been very agreeable, Gray would have shrunk from taking part in it. For him, relations with his fellows should always be private individual affairs, conducted, as it were, in a series of tête-à-tête interviews. Even if his friends knew each other, he preferred himself to see them separately. Mankind, in any corporate manifestation, was something to be avoided.

Such then was Gray's life: a deliberately worked-out plan, in which the different elements that pleased him in existence—study and idleness, solitude and friendship, nature and art—were blended together in balanced and temperate proportion. He put all his delicate sense of style into its execution. Artists' lives are often disillusioning to read about: for they are so surprisingly unaesthetic, so lacking in unity of design and harmony of tone, such a muddle of loose ends and false starts and jarring notes. Verlaine's life. Dostoieffsky's life, D. H. Lawrence's life—how could people so sensitive endure to live so tastelessly, one asks oneself. Perhaps the question is silly, perhaps the very explosive fire of their genius set them inevitably at odds with order and tame seemliness. All the same, Gray's life makes a pleasant contrast to theirs. Here all is in order, all is of a piece. In its own way it is as consummate a work of art as Horace Walpole's own.

Nor was it merely urbane and graceful. It was given depth and spirituality by the rich inner life of its creator. For this still went on. Behind the mask of the gentleman and the scholar, the poet dreamed and brooded. Though it was less disciplined and self-conscious than the life his fellows saw, Gray's inner life was in tune with it. There was nothing wild or unaccountable about it; and nothing visionary. The region of his dreams was a minor-key silver-tinted place, of reverie and pensive reflection and delicate half-smiling fancy. Nor did the contemplation of it ever carry him away to such an extent as to make him forget the existence of the external prosaic world. He knew his dreams were dreams: he did not take them so solemnly as to be unable lightly to make fun of them. His emotions about them never got out of the control of his reason. Indeed emotion and intellect played an equal part in his meditations. It was half of his satisfaction in them to analyse and discriminate the flights of his imagination, the impulses of his sensibility.

For, as always, his inner life was primarily concerned with his response to the beautiful. And, as always, this response was stimulated by two things, his feeling for nature, and sense of the historic past. Generally the two were blended together.

"In the bosom of the woods," he writes, "concealed from profane eyes—lie the ruins of Netley Abbey. There may be richer and greater houses of religion, but the abbot is content with his station. See there at the top of that hanging meadow, under the shade of those old trees that bend into a half-circle about it, he is walking slowly—good man! —and bidding his beads for the souls of his benefactors, interred on that venerable pile that lies beneath him. Beyond it—the meadow still descending—note a thicket of oaks, that mask the building and have excluded a view too garish and too luxuriant for a holy eye, only on either hand they leave an opening to the blue glittering sea. Did you not observe how, as that white sail shot by and was lost, he turned and crossed himself, to drive the Tempter from him, that had thrown that distraction in his way. I should tell you that the ferryman who rowed me, a lusty young fellow, told me that he would not for all the world pass a night at the Abbey—there were such things seen near it was thought there was a power of money hid there."

Was it the radiant landscape or its picturesque historical associations, that inspired this passage? The two are inextricably mixed: we cannot say. Similarly as he stood on the willowy banks of Cam in the first pale glow of a summer dawn, or, by night, paced the college cloisters where the tracery cast its intricate shadow, black on the moonlit pavement, his imagination was stirred half by the actual beauty of the scene and half by its power to conjure up before his mental eye the spectres of the illustrious dead who had walked there before him—monarchs, bishops, students, poets, stern Edward I, forlorn Henry VI, straddling Henry VIII, Newton and Milton absorbed in the ardent contemplations of their mighty youth.

> "High potentates, and dames of regal birth
> And mitred fathers in long order go:
> Great Edward, with the lilies on his brow
> From haughty Gallia torn,
> And sad Chatillon, on her bridal morn
> That wept her bleeding love, and princely Clare,
> And Angou's heroine, and the paler rose,
> True rival of her crown, and of her woes,
> And either Henry there.
> The murdered saint, and the majestic Lord
> That broke the bonds of Rome."

To Gray no place existed only in the present. Behind the England of his own day, he discerned as in a vision the long perspective of its past, peopled with figures of bygone generations, stretching away to the dim horizons of antiquity. As he wandered through the stone-paved great gallery of Hardwick Hall with its dim tapestries and sculptured chimneypieces, and beruffed inscrutable Tudor portraits, he could hardly believe that Mary, Queen of Scots, had not left it the moment before he entered: in the avenues of Warwick

Castle "the elms", he said, "seem to remember Sir Philip
Sidney, who often walked there—and talk of him to this
day." Music too was powerful to evoke Gray's sense of the
past. He was spellbound when the old Welsh harper Parry
sang the wild traditional ballads of his native land. The unintelligible words and irregular rhythms seemed to be the
very voice of the long-dead world of the Druids, echoing
strangely down the ages.

Natural sounds were not less active to stir his feelings and
his imagination. The singing of the young birds as he walked
with Nicholls one sunny spring day in the fields near Cambridge, caused his heart to rise involuntarily to carol with
them.

"There pipes the woodlark", so he improvised "and the
      song thrush there,
    Scatters her loose notes in the waste of air."

And the wail of the winter wind too, lamenting round the
chimneys on a winter night—"Did you never observe," he
cries, "that pause, as the gust is recollecting itself and rising up
on the ear in a shrill and plaintive note, like the swell of an
Aeolian harp? I do assure you there is nothing in the world so
like the voice of a spirit."

In this passage he speaks with a more impassioned accent
than when he is talking about Netley Abbey or the avenues
of Warwick. And, in fact, for all that his sense of history was
so strong, scenes of pure nature were the source of his intensest
and most profound spiritual experiences. All the more as he
grew older: it was as if, with the gradual failing of youthful
hope, and youthful energy, his spirit more and more sought
sustenance from the earth of which it was made and to which
it must decline. Not for nothing was botany the favourite
study of his later years. Descriptions of natural scenery take an
increasing space in the journals of his summer tours. With a

tireless concentration, an extraordinary loving particularity, he lingers over their typical details: the shining reaches of Ullswater "just ruffled by the breeze enough to show it is alive"; a walk by the river Kent made memorable by the strange contrast of the bright calm evening weather with the roar of a cataract and the thumping from the hammer of an iron forge, hidden in the trees near by: Derwentwater at twilight, with the shadows of the mountains lengthening across the glassy water and the air so still that he could hear the murmur of a waterfall far away in the distance; the pastoral charm of Grasmere, its banks broken into little bays, their outlines half hiding, half revealing the gleaming lake, and with a promontory jutting out into it, where a village and church clustered together, white against the emerald turf. "Not a single red tile," he mused, "no flaring gentleman's house or garden walls break in on the repose of this unsuspected little paradise, but all is peace, rusticity, and happy poverty in its neatest most becoming attire."

Sometimes nature disturbed a deeper chord in him. Never as long as he lived would he forget, so he said, the shuddering awe that possessed him, as he stood, one chill and gloomy afternoon, in the savage gorge of Gordale Scar, his cheek wet with the spray from a torrent that thundered foaming down from a rocky precipice frowning six hundred feet above his head: what a sense of glory and wonder flooded his heart when he chanced to witness the sun rise over the sea one summer morning on the Hampshire coast.

"I must not close my letter without giving you one principal event of my history; which was, that—in the course of my late tour—I set out one morning before 5 o'clock, the moon shining through a dark and misty autumnal air, and got to the sea-coast time enough to be at the sun's levee. I saw the clouds and dark vapours open gradually to right and left, rolling over one another in great smoky wreaths; and the tide—as it flowed in gently upon the sands—first whitening, then gently tinged with gold and blue: and all at once a little line of insufferable brightness that, before I can write these fine words, was grown to half an orb, and now to a whole one, too glorious to be distinctly seen. It is very odd, it makes no figure upon paper: yet I shall remember it as long as the sun, or at least as long as I endure. I wonder whether anybody ever saw it before? I can hardly believe it."

This description illustrates perfectly the individual distinguishing quality of Gray's imaginative life. Precisely he discerns the features in the scene that give it its character: exquisitely he responds to its sentiment. Yet it never sweeps him right away in a Ruskinian rhapsody of lyrical ecstasy. His tone of voice remains a conversational *prose* tone: and the little quip that closes the passage expresses, as it were, the smiling shrug with which, after his brief flight into the empyraean, he brings himself down to firm earth once more.

Thus Gray's instinct for harmony extended to the relation between his inner and outer life. They were not inconsistent. All the same they were different. The solitary Gray is a more impressive personality than the sociable. Gone are the timidity and suspiciousness that hamper and deform his relations with his fellows. Instead his sensibility, his imagination, his deep capacity for feeling, soar up, unalloyed and unimpeded, to their fulfilment. So that narrow and artificial as his mode of living might seem, the impression it leaves on us is not one of artificiality and narrowness. For he himself was too continually in touch with the majestic processes of the elemental earth, too profoundly aware of the transience and insignificance of the individual life in comparison with the huge dimension of past time. As in a canvas of Gainsborough, the

silken formal figure stands out before us shaded by the trees
of the woodland and against a dreamy illimitable distance.

Once or twice he allowed his inner life to disclose itself to
the world in a poem. In veiled fashion though; never again
was he to open his heart, as in the months after West's death.
The two great odes—The Bard and The Progress of Poesy—
which are the chief poetic achievement of these later years are
ceremonious, impersonal productions in which he hardly
mentions himself or his own feelings. But they are inspired
by matter drawn from his lonely contemplations and vivified
by the spirit that infused them. Intensely enough to awake a
response in his readers; they confirmed and increased his
fame. In 1757 Gray was offered the Poet Laureateship. This
however he at once and emphatically refused. His life was to
be a private life: writing was no more than one of his diversions: he was not going to set up as a professional author. As a
matter of fact it would have been difficult for him to, considering how little he produced. Only seven or eight not
very long poems in thirty years: and some of these he never
finished. As for bringing any prose work to a conclusion, he
found that impossible. The Edition of Strabo, the History
of English poetry, all those projects, so carefully meditated,
so sedulously prepared for—none of them got further than
his note-books.

From time to time Gray lamented this inability to finish:
but without much hope of curing it. Indeed its causes were
beyond his control. They were partly physical. Gray had
never been strong: in middle life he became sickly. A gouty
tendency, inherited from his father—his father seems to have
been a disaster to him in every way—began to manifest
itself, now in headaches, now in constipations, now in violent
fits of dizziness. These afflictions were not very serious.
But while they lasted, they prostrated him. And even when
he was free from them, he felt lethargic. All this sapped his

energy for concentrated work. Nine days out of ten he simply did not feel up to it. It was not only bad health, however, that inhibited him. Psychological causes also played their part. He was morbidly nervous of failure, morbidly sensitive to criticism. This last he would have denied. He was always protesting and declaring that he did not mind what other people thought of his work. But the very unnecessary emphasis with which he insists on his indifference suggests that it was, in part at least, assumed. Moreover, as we have seen, he liked sending his poems, while they were still in process of composition, round to his friends, that he might have a chance of remedying any defect they might complain of in them, before they were irretrievably launched on the world. Not that he would have altered anything in them against his own better judgment, just because someone else did not like it: he was too disinterestedly an artist for that. But the meticulous attention he paid to his friends' suggestions shows that he was not at all the sort of man who is completely satisfied so long as he has pleased himself. Here was something to inhibit still further his creative impulse. The standard of perfection he set himself was so high, and involved such a labour of polishing and re-writing that it was very seldom he felt strong enough to make the effort necessary for it. No—creative work was not for him. With relief, with despondency, with a tired, obstinate defiance he relaxed back to his routine of reading and note-taking and idle, aimless meditation.

"It is indeed for want of spirits, as you suspect," he told Wharton, "that my studies lie among the cathedrals and the tombs and the ruins. To think, though to little purpose, has been the chief amusement of my days: and when I would not, or cannot think, I dream. At present I find myself able to write a catalogue, or read the Peerage book, or Miller's *Gardening Dictionary*; and am thankful that there

are such employments and such authors in the world.
Some people who hold me cheap for this are doing perhaps
what is not half so well worth while. As to posterity, I may
ask—with somebody who I have forgot—what has it ever
done to oblige me?"

This incapacity to work was the sign of a deeper and more
general malady of spirit. It was the old trouble. He still
suffered from the fear of l fe. It showed itself every day of his
existence. He was haunted by morbid unreasonable apprehensions. Heights frightened him; so did dogs, so did horses.
In that age of horsemen, he never brought himself to learn to
ride. If he had to cross the water, he at once fancied he was
going to be drowned. After a rough crossing over the Firth
of Forth, he went thirty-five miles round on the return journey
rather than risk such an ordeal again. Fire was worse than
water. In 1758 he became filled with terror lest a fire should
break out in College; and that, living, as he did, four storeys
up, he should be trapped by it. Immediately he took elaborate precautions for his safety: had a horizontal iron bar fixed
outside his window with a rope-ladder, specially procured
from London, attached to it. Away from Cambridge, the
same fear possessed him. "'Tis strange," he wrote from
London once, "that all of us here in town lay ourselves down
every night on our funeral pile and compose ourselves to
rest: while every drunken footman and drowsy old woman
has a candle ready to light it before morning." Thieves were
another source of anxiety. He could not get off a parcel without fearing it might get stolen before it reached its destination.
When he had to send luggage ahead, he marked every item
in it according to an elaborate system of crosses and letters, so
that he should at once be able to recognize if everything had
arrived safely. Things might also get broken: here was another
anxiety. To assuage it, he insisted on his possessions being

carefully packed in straw and paper. But this precaution, in its turn, revived an old terror. Paper and straw were inflammable. Supposing a careless servant left a lighted candle about in the room in which he had been unpacking! It seemed impossible to be safe from one danger without involving oneself in another.

Such a temperament was not likely to take ill-health placidly. And indeed from middle life Gray was a confirmed hypochondriac; watching every slight up-and-down of his health with the microscopic concentration of a scientist conducting an important experiment. Here was occasion for a new set of notebooks and classified lists. Daily Gray set down the mournful catalogue of his aches and eye-troubles and digestive disturbances, together with that of the remedies he took to alleviate them. He dieted, he gave up wine, he never went for a walk in the wind without wrapping up his face in a shawl. Even if for once he was not feeling ill, he continued to worry. Was he not, he asked himself, feeling like someone who is shortly going to feel ill? Suffering from a definite ailment was in some ways a relief: then at least he was free from the pains of suspense.

Mental dangers troubled as much as physical. Seeing his lawyer, doing his accounts, going on a journey—all these were liable to set him worrying. Going on a journey was particularly agitating: it often is to neurotic persons. For days before he started, Gray was in a state of anxiety. Would he be ready in time? Would he remember to leave his address behind? Getting off did not always calm him. Once when he was travelling, he got news that an important-looking letter had arrived for him, at Cambridge. At once he began to rack his brains as to what might be in it. There was no peace of mind for him till it was safely in his hands.

But it was in his relations with other people that his nervousness showed itself most forcibly. The seclusion in which he now lived made him more painfully shy than ever, if he did find himself forced by unlucky chance into company. During a visit to a sociable hotel at Malvern during the Season he did not speak for a week: Lady Ailesbury told Walpole that once when she had managed to persuade him to come on a day's picnic party, he only opened his mouth once. "Yes, My Lady, I think so," he murmured, and then relapsed into an unbroken silence. No wonder the voluble Walpole got irritated with him. How could such a master of words as he knew Gray to be, endure to be such a wet blanket! Gray could not help it: society merely made him feel inadequate and depressed. And the merrier it was, the gloomier he became. "People in high spirits and gaiety overpower me," he said to Wharton, "and entirely take away mine. I can yet be diverted with their sallies, but if they take notice of my dullness, it sinks me to nothing." In the effort to cover up his shyness, he involuntarily exaggerated his supercilious artificiality of manner. The consequence was that he did not make a good impression on strangers. Obscurely he felt this; and became stiffer than ever. But things were hardly better at Cambridge, where he was not among strangers. The average don found him very uncomfortable company: while the undergraduates could not conceal their laughter at the finicky figure with its tottery walk and wrapped-up face and ridiculous fears and fads. At one time poor Gray even became a recognized object of undergraduate jokes. He was not the man to take this in good part, especially as undergraduate jokes in the eighteenth century were on the crude side. Indeed they were the cause of an event that, in a life so preternaturally quiet as Gray's, can only be called sensational. It occurred in 1759. Some rooms on his staircase were occupied by two horsey young men of fashion, Mr. Williams and Mr. Forrester. When they were feeling particularly high-spirited, they worked it off by playing pranks on Gray, and waking him up in the middle of the night by the noise they made. Gray complained to the authorities; but the authorities did not receive his complaints with much sympathy. Gray grew very annoyed. The climax was reached very early one March morning when Mr. Williams and Mr. Forrester in company with a friend of their's, young Lord Percival, were starting off for a day's hunting. Passing below Gray's rooms, they noticed the iron bar he had erected against fire. It was, we must admit, a considerable temptation to anyone with a taste for practical joking. "Let's make Gray bolt!" they said: and accordingly they sent Lord Percival's servant to go upstairs and bellow "Fire!" outside Gray's door as loud as he could, in the hope of luring Gray down the ladder so that they could, as they put it, "whip the butterfly up again". The plot seemed as if it were going to succeed: in due course a pale face surmounted by a silken nightcap was seen, in the grey dimness of dawn, peering agitatedly out of the window. Suddenly, however, it was withdrawn. Gray had caught sight of the upturned faces of his tormentors in time to avoid delivering himself into their hands.

He cannot be said to have suffered any very dreadful experience, by ordinary standards. But to a man with his tendency to persecution mania, it was the last straw. He tore off to the Master of Peterhouse clamouring for vengeance on the perpetrators of so shocking an insult to his dignity. What was his sense of outrage when the Master pooh-poohed the whole affair as "a young man's frolic"? Not for a day longer was Gray going to demean himself by remaining in such a bear garden. He resigned his fellowship. How far he thought this involved the drastic step of leaving Cambridge altogether we do not know. Anyway there was no question of this. For Pembroke just over the way, where his friend Brown was a Fellow, offered to take him in. A month later we find him writing from there to his friends telling them that, for reasons too tedious to go into, he had left Peterhouse. When they discovered the truth, these friends praised his magnanimity in not mentioning the real cause of his departure. Perhaps, though, his silence was due to another reason; perhaps he was afraid that if he did mention it, he would look a little silly.

After this his troubles seem to have stopped. There is no record of any unseemly practical jokes being played on him at Pembroke. But he did not become more sociable. On the contrary, during his last years he lived more retired a life than ever. He was by now one of the most famous of living writers. Yet when he took his daily walk to the Botanical gardens, hardly anyone recognized him.

There was nothing very new in all this however. Gray never had got on with strangers. But now even his relations with his small cluster of close friends had become a touch inhibited. It came partly from an inevitable clash between his temperament and his mode of living. Instinctively he still craved an intense relationship; by nature he longed to be first in another's affections. But this could not be done without entangling his life with theirs. And the whole aim of his scheme of existence was to be free of entanglement. Entanglement would upset the regular order of his days: worse, it was a threat to the security of such peace of mind as he had managed to achieve. Never again did he wish to suffer as he had over West and Walpole. Anyway he was, for the time being at any rate, incapable of the self-surrender required for that kind of friendship: he had not the confidence in other human beings that it implied. Here was where his fear of life showed itself. His reserve now spread itself over the whole surface of his personality. He lived within the system of solitary habit he had erected for himself, as in a locked citadel. At regular intervals, it pleased him to sally forth and enjoy the delights of an hour's conversation with a sympathetic spirit. But when it was over, he went back: nor did he ever take anyone in with him. To none of his friends did he write as openly and intimately as he had to West. And though he was too sensible to quarrel, he was if anything more critical than before. With detached clarity, he noticed his friends' faults; so that his affections though genuine and constant, were not glowingly warm. The full free current of his impulse to love was checked.

Sometimes it pretty well dried up. This was what happened with Miss Speed. She can never have understood him very well: for on one occasion we find her reproaching him, on the extraordinary ground that he paid insufficient attention to his health. Most likely she was under the not uncommon delusion that poets are impractical, up-in-the-clouds creatures, incapable of running their own lives: and only too grateful that an efficient female friend, like herself for instance, should take on the job for them. This was the last sort of thing Gray wanted. However Miss Speed did not get much chance to try it: and for some years their relationship jogged along comfortably enough. Then in 1760 Lady Cobham died, leaving her the heiress to thirty thousand pounds, a house in London, and a great deal of china. Rendered confident by these advantages, she began to display her dominating bent more clearly. At once and with displeasure, Gray noticed it. She asked him to stay with her, but then changed the date of his visit several times to suit her whim, a most disturbing thing to a man who liked to know his exact plans months beforehand. And then when he did arrive, she plunged him into a vortex of social activity. "I am come to my resting-place," he wrote tartly once he was safe back at Cambridge, "and find it very necessary after living for a month in a house with three women, that laughed from morning to night and would allow nothing to the sulkiness of my disposition. Company and cards at home, parties by land and water; and what they call *doing something*, that is racketting about from morning to night, are occupations, I find, that wear out my spirits: especially in a situation where one might sit and be alone, with pleasure." It is not surprising that, as far as we know, he did not visit her again.

How Miss Speed took his defection we are not told. It was rumoured that she had hoped to marry him. This seems unlikely seeing that she was, by all accounts, of a shrewd cool temperament, and as such, not at all the woman to fix her affections on someone so unlikely to return them. In any case, she soon cut her losses. In 1761 she married the Baron de la Perrière, a Sardinian nobleman, six years younger than herself, and left England to settle in Switzerland. Considering that this must have seemed likely to mean permanent separation from her, Gray heard it very philosophically. "My old friend Miss Speed has done what the world calls a very foolish thing," he said, ". . . what she has done with her money I know not: but—I suspect—kept it to herself." When however four years later she came back to England on a visit, he called on her. "She has grown a prodigious fine lady," he told Wharton, "and a Catholic—though she did not expressly own it to me: not fatter than she was. She had a cage of foreign birds and a piping bullfinch at her elbow, two little dogs on a cushion in her lap, a cockatoo on her shoulder and a slight suspicion of rouge on her cheeks." Though he professed himself to have been very pleased to see her, this description is more satirical than affectionate. Gray was not going to forget that Miss Speed could be very tiresome.

Chute, too, seems in the end to have lost Gray's friendship. For some years Gray often stayed with him enjoying pleasant talks about music and invalid symptoms. But, after 1760, Chute's name disappears from the list of Gray's correspondents. Presumably he had said or done something—we do not know what—which had made Gray strike him off the

carefully selected list. Even of Walpole—as we have seen—
he could at times be very critical. The only people with whom
his relations were calm and stable were his young disciples
and solid old friends like Brown and Wharton. But Brown
and Wharton had never been the object of his intenser romantic sentiment: while the difference of age and position between
himself and his disciples kept them always at a cool respectful
distance from him. Never, once he had settled into maturity,
did he achieve a friendship that fully satisfied the demands of
his nature. Always there was something strained, or something lacking.

No—in spite of all his care and judgment and self-discipline, Gray failed to find that solid tranquillity of spirit
which above all things he longed for. It was impossible he
should. To avoid the suffering which had blighted his youth,
he had taken refuge in a universe of his own, constructed to
exclude the occasion of anything that might give him pain.
But pain, alas, is an ineradicable constituent of human existence. It comes primarily from within: and is at least as much
due to character as to circumstance. Certainly this was true
of Gray. He was constitutionally languid, temperamentally
melancholy; and early education had left him incurably the
prey to a neurotic fear of life. These weaknesses were bound
to affect him whatever his mode of living. If his neurosis
did not find a big thing to nourish itself on, it fed upon a small
one: if he had nothing else to worry about, he worried about
losing his luggage. He had erected elaborate defences against
the assault of outside events, only to discover that, like Sir
Thomas Browne, he had Lucifer and all his angels within
him. Nor, as a matter of fact, did his defences turn out to be
impervious against external enemies. Gray was, he could not
help being, an artist with all the artist's lightning responsiveness to the mental atmosphere of the world around him. It
was no use his saying that he thought so poorly of mankind

that he despised its opinion. The fact remained that, as we have seen, when the undergraduates laughed at him, he felt outraged: and that when Walpole proposed using his portrait as the frontispiece to his poems, he was in a fever lest it should make him appear a fool in the eyes of his readers. He even refused to take a degree, for fear he should be confused with another Dr. Gray, who had made himself ridiculous by publishing a worthless edition of Hudibras. The proud contempt for mankind and its ignoble preoccupations which he professed to be his motive for retiring from the arena of active life, was not serene and self-sufficient, but a strained, nervous, vulnerable affair, and in part at least, a cover to hide his shrinking from the pain and mortification in which he feared that a struggle might involve him.

"Too poor for a bribe," so he wrote of himself,
    "and too proud to importune,
    He had not the method of making a fortune."

He had not the nerve either.

Moreover, Gray's mode of living did lay him open to some peculiar dangers. It tended to weaken such little energy as he possessed. To work, if you do not have to, is always hard and needs a more forceful character than Gray's. He only embarked on any creative work if the mood took him. And, since he did nothing to induce such a mood, it took him less and less often. The eventless regular round of his days, as they ticked slowly away amid the sequestered college courts, was profoundly unstimulating. He was, as it were, becalmed. Further, so much of his vitality was occupied in warding off disaster, that there was little left for anything else. With the harsh invigorating gale of the world excluded carefully from every cranny, the mental atmosphere in which he lived grew airless and exhausted; his spirit began to flag even from those activities which he enjoyed. He felt no heart for writing: his talent for friendship was checked of fulfilment. If a man rejects life, life soon begins to reject him.

All the same Gray did not make a mistake in living as he did. He was faced with a choice of evils. And he chose the lesser. He simply could not have stood the strain of an active life: it would have entailed his acting perpetually against the whole bias of his nature. The consequence could only have been collapse. The life he did choose, on the other hand, was in accordance with this bias. And, when all is said and done, he got more pleasure than pain out of it. Moreover the pain was moderated by the exercise of those qualities that had served him so well in previous crises: his fortitude, his irony, his unegotistic good sense. Though he could not overcome his weaknesses, he recognized them as such, and made no attempt to excuse them. Neither did he yield to the temptation to indulge in self-pity. Except in moments of extreme agitation, he speaks of his own fears and fusses with something of the same amusement as he would speak of other people's follies. And he took care always to remind himself that his troubles were most likely no worse than those the rest of the world had to put up with: and, as such, could and should be endured without complaint. "A life," he told Mason in one of his letters of paternal advice, "spent out of the world has its hours of despondence, its inconveniences, its sufferings as numerous and as real—though not quite of the same sort— as a life spent in the midst of it. The power we have, when we will exert it, over our own minds, joined to a little strength and consolation, nay a little pride, caught from those that seem to love us, is our only support in either of those conditions. . . . I can only tell you that one that has far more reason than you, I hope, will ever have, to look on life with something worse than indifference, is yet no enemy to it; and can look back on many bitter moments partly with satisfaction and partly with patience; and forward too, on a scene not very promising, with some hope and some expectations of a better day." Sometimes he even wondered if a certain amount of suffering was not necessary to joy. Perhaps pleasure was only acute when it came as a contrast to preceding pain.

"The hues of bliss more brightly glow
   Chastised by sabler tints of woe," he sang,
"And, blended, form with artful strife
   The strength and harmony of life.

See the wretch that long has tost
   On the thorny bed of pain,
At length repair his vigour lost
   And breathe and walk again:

The meanest flowret of the vale,
The simplest note that swells the gale,
The common sun, the air, the skies,
To him are opening Paradise."

Indeed Gray's life, as it rises before us from letter and poem, was nothing to be ashamed of. It is highly creditable surely for a man to make his existence into a finished work of art in which, to outward appearance at any rate, all is dignity and order, harmony and grace, and whose every manifestation bears the signature of an exquisite and individual taste. That it should not always have succeeded in making its creator perfectly happy is a pity; and stirs melancholy reflections on the incorrigibly unsatisfactory nature of the human lot. But it should not lead us to condemn Gray. Rather must he be praised for producing something so admirable in face of such difficulties. Moreover his creative impulse was not completely frustrated. Unintentionally it found expression in the carefully composed letters which he despatched with regularity to his friends. Not that those letters were unaffected by his inhibitions. That they were reserved was to be expected; but they were also unspontaneous and a little impersonal. One misses the sound of the speaking voice, the ardent unselfconscious intimacy of tone which marks Dorothy's letters, even at their most ceremonious. Still, Gray's are classics of their kind, as perfect examples of English eighteenth century taste as a Chippendale cabinet, and with the same mixture of elegance and substance. For even at their lightest, there is usually a firm centre of intelligence and information to them, some penetrating literary judgment, some shrewd comment on character or affairs. Yet all is charming, all is easy; and ever and again the page glitters with a stylish caustic stroke of wit or glows to beauty as in musical cadence and precise delicate phrase, he discloses some picturesque vista or indulges in a flight of airy fancy. The author of such letters cannot be said to have wholly failed to fulfil his talents. And he must have known the happiness that comes from such fulfilment.

On the whole too, he grew happier as time passed. The hope of better days he expressed to Mason was not unfounded. In spite of recurrent intervals of depression, the middle-aged Gray was more serene than he had been since boyhood. Circumstances had something to do with this. The death of his aunt in 1758 made him both richer and freer. Not only could he spend his summers wandering about to see as many abbeys and beauty spots as he felt inclined instead of stagnating at Stoke Poges, but he was able to engage a manservant of his own to help him in the arduous task of looking after the luggage and the medicines. So inspirited did he begin to feel that in the summer of 1759, when he was toying with the idea of writing his *History of English Poetry*, he took the unprecedented step of setting up his headquarters in London for three years, in order to research in the British Museum. Not that his mode of living there was very different from what it had been at Cambridge. He found some quiet comfortable rooms in Jermyn Street, filled them with such flowers as were in season—we get a glimpse of his sitting-room one July, all gay with scarlet Martagon lilies and flowering marjoram—and settled down to a life of retirement and study. All day he worked at the British Museum; and in the afternoon dined off a choice little meal, sent in from a neighbouring tavern, alone or in the company of a chosen friend, with whom he sipped a glass or two of sweet wine and, "as he sipped, talked of great people". His circle of friends was growing at this time—this was another reason that he was happier. It was round about now that he collected most of his young disciples. In the sunshine of their admiration, his spirits softened and brightened. His prevailing mood became mellower; the tone of his letters is more playful: now and again he even broke out in one of those flights of exuberant fantastic humour which had characterized him in the first carefree days of the Quadruple Alliance. Once—this was after he had returned to Cambridge—he was persuaded to write an ode on the Installation of the Duke of Grafton as Chancellor of the University. Nicholls called on him while it was in process of composition. What was his astonishment when Gray flung open the door exclaiming in loud and hollow tones "Hence avaunt! 'tis holy ground!" For a moment Nicholls felt a spasm of alarm. He knew Gray well enough to realize his nervous instability. How dreadful if he had suddenly gone off his head! It was a relief to find he was only reciting the first lines of the ode he was writing.

Finally, to his growing private happiness was added the gratification of public recognition. In 1768 Gray was made Regius Professor of History at Cambridge. This was a most agreeable job; £400 a year with only nominal duties attached to it. Gray had long hankered after the Professorship; so much so that in 1762 he had broken his rule of life, and applied for it. He was refused. When in 1768 it had again become vacant, he did not risk the humiliation of a second refusal. This made it all the more delightful to get a letter offering it to him; and in the most flattering terms. He accepted at once. There was one more hurdle to be negotiated before he could relax to enjoy the sweets of the position undisturbed. He had to pay a ceremonial visit of acknowledgment at Court. He made as heavy weather of this as might have been expected. His manner, it was noted, exhibited more than ever his usual mixture of shyness and superciliousness: himself, he felt so overcome that he did not know who was talking to him or what they said. Conscious that he had not cut an impressive figure in the presence of his Sovereign, Gray became noticeably ill-humoured whenever the subject was mentioned to him. However, this was a very small spot on a brilliant sun. Gray wrote round to tell his friends the news together with the compliments he had received about it, in an airy off-hand manner which did not conceal the exhilaration with which it filled him. Was he still so certain after all, the reader wonders, that the applause of mankind was not worth having?

Gray only lived for three more years after this. It would be pleasant to relate that his spirits maintained their improvement to the end of his life. Alas, Fate proved too ruthlessly conscientious an artist to finish a tale so melancholy on an incongruously cheerful note. Nothing very catastrophic happened: catastrophe also would have been incongruous with Gray. But clouds arose to hide the temperate gleam of sunshine, which had for a short time irradiated him, and the evening of his days was grey and troubled. Ironically the first cloud was caused by the event which, when it came, had promised to bring him such unalloyed pleasure, his appointment to the Professorship. One of its chief attractions had been that it appeared to involve no work: his predecessors, most of them, had gone through their term of office without lecturing to anyone. Unluckily, however, the autumn of 1768 saw the outbreak of one of those regrettable and ineffective impulses to self-improvement which arise from time to time to disturb the serenity of University life. It happened at Oxford. People there began saying that the Professor of History really did not do enough to earn his salary; some revolutionary spirits went so far as to demand that he should be required to give fifty lectures a year. The noise of the agitation penetrated to London: government circles became interested and began to make formal inquiries as to what should be done. Gray was asked, in his new official capacity, to give his opinion. Reluctantly he found himself forced by his conscience to say that a professor ought to do something: perhaps he should lecture, if not fifty, at any rate three times a year. After this the agitation seems to have died down: for the Oxford professor went on for the rest of his life happily giving no lectures at all. But the fact that the question had arisen had been enough to destroy Gray's precarious peace of mind. Not only did he suspect—groundlessly as it happened—that everyone was criticizing him for idleness behind his back, but he became a prey to the pangs of his fretting, scrupulous conscience. Even if no-one minded, was he justified in receiving £400 on what, if he had been offered it two years later, might possibly have been considered false pretences? Painfully and without enthusiasm he began preparing an inaugural lecture. It was conceived on a formidable scale; embracing as it did one section on the study of history, another on the study of the sources of history and a third on the study of those subjects necessary to prepare oneself for studying the sources of history. Clearly all his notebooks should be called into use to provide information for such a task. Gray rendered his task even more laborious by deciding that he ought to write it in Latin,

a language in the composition of which he had lately grown
rather rusty. It was not to be expected that he, who for
twenty years had found it difficult to complete a short poem,
should accomplish a labour of this kind. Alike his inhibitions
and his standard of perfection made it impossible: months
passed without the lecture getting further than the first sketch.
Nobody at Cambridge seemed to notice. But Gray did. He
could not get it out of his head. To his other neuroses was
added a gnawing sense of guilt.

He was in no state of mind to stand an emotional crisis. And
now suddenly, after nearly thirty years, he was required to
face one, as violent, in its own way, as that which succeeded
West's death. In the November of 1769, Nicholls, who was
staying at Bath, went to a ball at the Assembly Rooms. In
order to get a better view of the dancers he climbed on to a
table. In doing so, he knocked against a young man who,
with the same purpose in view, was climbing on to it from
the other side. The contretemps led to apologies, apologies to
acquaintance. The stranger turned out to be a foreigner, a
twenty-one-year-old Swiss called Bonstetten, who was
paying a visit to England. Nicholls took to him at once.
Small and handsome with delicate colouring, expressive mouth,
and bright eyes "full of a smiling sweetness", he combined
the ease and polish of one accustomed to the best society with
an electric foreign vitality, all aquiver with sensibility. In a
flood of attractively broken English, he poured out about the
enthusiastic feelings stirred in him by the Alpine scenery of his
native land, with its towering sombre pine glades, to whose
atmosphere the cry of a distant eagle added a pleasing horror.
All this was thoroughly in the taste of the Gray circle. Nicholls
wrote off at once to Gray saying he simply must get to know
him. A month later, Gray, while staying for a day or two in
London, took the opportunity to follow his advice. He was
even more struck than Nicholls had been. So much so that

forgetting his usual diffidence, he persuaded Bonstetten to come down to Cambridge on a visit. Closer acquaintance did not prove disappointing. Indeed his new friend, if a trifle absurd sometimes, was a genuinely engaging and original personality. Charles Victor de Bonstetten was the son of an ancient aristocratic family residing in the Canton of Berne. From his earliest years he had shown himself clever, vital and mercurial—too much so to feel at home in the prim and prosaic atmosphere of Berne society. However at the age of fifteen he was sent to finish his education in Geneva, then a minor centre of European social and intellectual life. Here he blossomed. He entered with delight into society, the civilized little evening parties where he quickly learnt to sparkle, flirt and pay compliments: still more he took to the new Romantic fashion in thought and feeling—all mountains and ruins and tender sentiments and rebellious noble aspirations—which, under the influence of Rousseau, was now sweeping Europe. He dreamed of a life which—while retaining the gaiety and elegance of a high civilization—was yet dedicated to the worship of Virtue, Liberty and the Ideal. These words, indeed, were seldom off his lips. After the delights of Geneva, Berne, where he returned in 1767 to start on a professional career, seemed to him more intolerably philistine than ever. In fact he became so depressed by it that, in approved Romantic fashion, he threatened suicide. His parents, alarmed at the new vagary on the part of their brilliant and unaccountable offspring, were only too willing to accept an alternative suggestion, that he should complete his education by a little foreign travel. Accordingly, after a short stay in Holland—he disliked the Dutch who seemed to him as uninspiring as the Bernese themselves—he found himself in England. Here his spirits soared up as high as they had sunk in Berne. The English were extremely friendly: they were also extraordinary—extraordinary in Bath, extraordinary in London, extraordinary above all at Cambridge. To his up-to-date continental eye, it seemed as if he had been wafted back three centuries into some monastery of the Middle Ages. He could not get over the strangeness of the cavernous Gothic halls and shadowy echoing stone cloisters through which young gentlemen, disguised as monks in long dark gowns, flitted, quite content apparently to live for weeks deprived of those pleasures of the Beau Monde, to which their birth gave them the entrée. And such social life as the place did provide, was even odder: slow ceremonious morning calls where dowdy ladies and solemn begowned dons sat in a circle, sometimes silent for a quarter of an hour at a time and then—this struck Bonstetten as peculiarly astonishing—only speaking when they had something to say. He thought of trying to brighten the party by making himself agreeable in the Geneva style—returning a handkerchief she had dropped to a lady with a graceful compliment, or saying something civil to a gentleman: but he refrained. He saw he would only embarrass.

However if Cambridge social life was stiff, it was, unlike that of Berne, eccentrically, fascinatingly stiff. Besides, the place had other things to offer to a man with Bonstetten's intellectual aspirations. He threw himself into making the most of them, took lessons in every sort of subject from botany to Italian, and cultivated the society of Gray. He went in for intellectual hero-worship—it was part of his "Romantic" rôle —and already in Switzerland he had sat at the feet of M. Haller the philosopher. Never would he forget how inspiring it had been to sit in M. Haller's library watching him write his letters, read the English newspaper and conduct a valuable discussion on the nature of free-will, all at the same moment. When he learnt that Gray was generally regarded as the greatest living English poet, Bonstetten determined to fling himself at his feet too.

Gray was only too willing that he should. He had always

liked enthusiastic pupils: but never had he met a pupil, never since he grew up, had he met anyone who had attracted him so immediately. Bonstetten was all that Gray liked most. For to that blend of gay aristocratic stylishness with sensibility and love of learning which had originally enchanted him in Walpole, he added a faculty of poetic enthusiasm and a warm foreign demonstrativeness, of which the satirical and worldly-wise Walpole was quite incapable; and which, like a burst of sunshine melted the film of ice which for so long had enclosed Gray's shivering heart. On to Bonstetten flowed out all the dammed-up unused emotion of years. It was the stronger and sweeter because it was so long since Gray had permitted himself anything of the kind. And it had a peculiar poignancy because, unlike his sentiment for the friends of his youth, there was a streak of the paternal in it. The frustrated father in Gray went out to Bonstetten, making him yearn to guide his steps, to protect his fresh innocence against the corruptions of the wicked world. Within a few weeks his liking for Bonstetten had swelled into an obsessing affection. He could not think or talk of anything else. He was intoxicated. And transfigured: his fear of letting himself go, his anxiety lest the order of his life should be upset, vanished almost in a night. Bonstetten, it is interesting to note, alone of his friends, seems to have been unaware that Gray could appear stiff or forbidding. For with him Gray never did. On the contrary he pressed him to come and see him every hour of the day. At first Bonstetten had not liked to call before five in the evening. But soon the two were together from breakfast on. They walked together, read together—if Bonstetten had some work of his own to do, he came and did it in Gray's room—had their meals together, made music together, even wrote letters together. "I am in a hurry from morning till evening," so Bonstetten will write off to Nicholls, "at 8 o'clock I am roused by a young square-cap with whom I follow Satan through chaos and night. He explained me in Greek and Latin the *sweet reluctant amorous delays* of our grandmother Eve. We finish our travels in a copious breakfast of muffins and tea. Then appears Shakespair and old Lineus struggling together as two ghosts would do for a damned soul. Sometimes the one gets the better, sometimes the other. Mr. Gray, whose acquaintance is my greatest debt to you, is so good as to show me Macbeth and all witches, beldams, ghost and spirits, whose language I should never have understood without his interpretation. I am now endeavouring to dress all those people in a french dress which is a very hard labour. I am afraid to take a room, which Mr. Gray shall keep still better. So I stop hier my everrambling pen." As he put down his ever-rambling pen, Gray took it up. "I never saw such a boy: our breed is not made on this model. He is busy from morning to night, has no other amusement than that of changing one study for another, likes nobody he sees here, and yet wishes to stay longer, though he has passed a whole fortnight with us already. His letter has no corrections whatever, and is prettier by half than English."

It is indeed a change to find Gray so uncritically delighted by anyone. It is also a change to find him so bewildered. Bonstetten's displays of temperament, the way he yielded himself completely to every passing mood, struck the inhibited Gray as so extraordinary that sometimes he wondered if his young friend was quite sane. But this suspicion of exotic lunacy only added an exhilarating strangeness to his charm. Nor was this charm always so volatile. Bonstetten could be beautifully quiet. Of an evening especially: delicious unforgettable evenings when, with the chill January night shut out by curtains and the wail of the wind, as it blew over the surrounding fen country, only serving to emphasize by contrast the warm security of the candlelit room, Gray dreamed by the fire while Bonstetten's fingers strayed softly over the keys of the pianoforte; or Bonstetten lay stretched on the sofa pouring forth into Gray's sympathetic ear all the secrets and troubles and aspirations of his youthful heart, or listened with eyes aglow as, in measured tones and picked felicitous phrase, Gray discoursed of Shakespeare and Milton and the classical languages and the course of English history and the folly of atheism. Of everything but himself: Bonstetten noticed that if he asked Gray anything about his own life and past history, he became at once, and strangely, silent. He also remarked that through the surface sparkle of Gray's talk was discernible a profound melancholy of spirit. Clearly there was some mystery about him; it piqued Bonstetten's lively inquisitiveness. His romantic spirit found a romantic explanation for it. "Gray n'avait jamais aimé," he said—Gray had never loved.

It is a cruelly ironical sentence, considering who uttered it. For, though Gray may well have been inhibited from loving in the conventional and physical sense of the word, his heart was very far from invulnerable. And who should have known it better than Bonstetten? The god of love is a vindictive deity: and seldom allows those who seek to evade his influence to go for ever unpunished. For twenty-eight years Gray had contrived by viligant care to keep his deeper emotions unstirred. And now at fifty-two he was the helpless victim of an infatuation as vain as it was irresistible. For what satisfaction could he hope for from a romantic attachment to a youth of twenty-two, restless, sociable, and whose home was in Switzerland? He could not even expect to see him often. Indeed within five weeks of his arrival in Cambridge, Bonstetten got a letter from his parents pressing him to come home. He had to obey them: and all the sooner because he wanted to see a little more of the world on his way back. Sorry as he was to leave his cher M. Gray, it seemed a pity to lose a chance of sampling the pleasures of Paris. For Bonstetten, once more like Walpole, liked parties and pretty women and being at the glittering centre of things. At the end of March, 1770, Gray accompanied him to London, in order to be with him up to the last possible moment. Two days later, in the mirk of a spring dawn, Bonstetten climbed into the Dover coach and said good-bye. Gray never saw him again.

He arrived back in Cambridge in a state of black depression such as he had not known for years. Everything in his life seemed suddenly to have lost its savour. He got no pleasure from reading or listening to music, or looking at flowers. The charming room, in which he had lived so long and on which he had lavished so much care, now served only to remind him at every turn, and agonisingly, of the happy hours he had spent there with Bonstetten. Bereft of that vivid life-enhancing figure, what was it but a place of dull lonely horror? It is extraordinary that eight short weeks should have effected such a revolution in his feelings. But those eight weeks had been the first for years in which Gray had lived with the full intensity of which his nature was capable. And, by contrast, all the long-established, carefully built-up structure of his existence, with its rigid habits and delicate, deliberate pleasures, now showed up as repulsively bloodless and empty. He cursed Cambridge—"Never has the place appeared so horrible to me as it does now!" he cried—cursed the selfish possessive love of parents, cursed himself. So miserable was he that for once his reserve showed signs of breaking. It was more that flesh and blood could bear to be silent. Seated at his writing table, he poured out to Bonstetten, in accents of trembling emotion quite unlike anything else in his correspondence, the utter desolation that filled his heart.

"Never did I feel, my dear Bonstetten, to what a tedious length the few short moments of our life may be extended

by impatience and expectation, till you had left me: nor
ever knew before with so strong a conviction how much
this frail body sympathizes with the inquietude of the mind.
I am grown old in a compass of less than three weeks, like
the Sultan in the Turkish tale, that did but plunge his head
into a vessel of water and take it out again—as the standers-
by affirmed, at the command of a Dervish, and found he
had passed many years in captivity and begot a large
family of children. The strength and spirits, that now
enable me to write to you are only owing to your last
letter—a temporary gleam of sunshine. Heaven knows
when it may shine again! I did not conceive till now, I
own, what it was to lose you, nor felt the solitude and insipidity of my own condition, before I possessed the happiness of your friendship."

And then a week later:

"Alas! how do I every moment feel the truth of what I
have somewhere read: *Ce n'est pas le voir que de s'en souvenir.*
And yet that remembrance is the only satisfaction I have
left. My life now is but a perpetual conversation with your
shadow—the known sound of your voice still rings in my
ears—there on the corner of the fender you are standing
or tinkling on the pianoforte or stretched at length on the
sofa. Do you reflect my dearest friend, that it is a week or
eight days before I can receive a letter from you, and as
much more before you can have my answer, that all the
time, with more than Herculean toil, I am employed in
pushing the tedious hours along and wishing to annihilate
them: the more I strive, the heavier they move and the
longer they grow. I cannot bear this place, where I have
spent many tedious years, within less than a month since
you left me. . . . You do me the credit—and, false or true,

it goes to my heart—of ascribing to me your love for many virtues of the highest rank. Would to heaven it were so! but they are indeed the fruits of your own noble and generous understanding, that has hitherto struggled against the stream of custom, passion and ill company, even when you were but a child. And will you now give way to that stream, when your strength is increased? Shall the jargon of French sophists, the allurements of painted women *comme il faut*, or the vulgar caresses of prostitute beauty, the property of all that can afford to purchase it, induce you to give up a mind and a body, by nature distinguished from all others, to folly, idleness, disease and vain remorse? Have a care, my ever amiable friend, of loving what you do not approve."

There is something comic in the agitated concern for Bonstetten's moral welfare, which Gray evinces in these last sentences. But it is highly illuminating in revealing the processes of his heart and feeling at this time. It was not just Bonstetten's physical absence that he minded: he also feared he might be going to lose him in a more permanent and spiritual sense. The Bonstetten he loved, the Bonstetten to whom alone he felt his friendship could be important, was the ingenuous boy on fire for education and enlightenment, who needed an older friend to whom he might unburden his soul and who asked no stronger pleasure than that provided by the innocent hours of talk and music by Gray's fireside. But now he was going out into the world, that world Gray had always shunned and feared. Worse still to Gray's sturdy British virtue, it was the world of eighteenth-century Paris, notorious, meretricious home-town of vice and Voltaire. Just because Bonstetten was so unusually attractive, it would do its best to corrupt him; just because he was so responsive, he would easily be tempted to yield to its seductions. The ingenuous boy would disappear, to be replaced by a man, cynical, superficial, godless, and licentious. It is significant how Gray harps on this last danger. Like so many confirmed celibates, he seems to have recoiled from sex as from something in itself repulsive and frightening, at any rate in its more animal manifestations: so that the mere thought of any connection between it and the beloved object struck him as indescribably revolting. Perhaps too he feared lest the intoxications of love would blunt Bonstetten's taste for the more ethereal pleasures of friendship. After the accomplished embraces of a Parisian woman of fashion, he might well find reading *Paradise Lost* with Gray a trifle insipid. Thus, disguised as moral disapproval, jealousy crept in to increase the dead weight of regret and loneliness and hopeless apathy that lay on Gray's breast.

So oppressive did it become that he found the solitude of his days at Cambridge intolerable. He wrote off to Nicholls imploring him to come down for a few days: "It would be sunshine to me in a dark night," he pleaded. Nicholls asked Gray to stay with him in Suffolk instead. Gray went, but found himself no more cheerful for it. After a fortnight he returned to Cambridge: and once more sat down to write to Bonstetten.

"I am returned, my dear Bonstetten, from the little journey I had made into Suffolk, without answering the end proposed. The thought that you might have been with me there has embittered all my hours. Your letter has made me happy; as happy as so gloomy, so solitary, a being as I am is capable of being. I know and have too often felt the disadvantages I lay myself under, how much I hurt the little interest I have in you, by this air of sadness so contrary to your nature and present engagements: but sure you will forgive me though you cannot sympathize with me. It is impossible with me to dissemble with you. Such as I am, I expose my heart to your view, nor wish to conceal a single thought from your penetrating eyes. All that you say to me, especially on the subject of Switzerland, is infinitely acceptable. It feels too pleasing ever to be fulfilled; and as often as I read over your truly kind letter written long since from London I stop at these words: 'La mort qui peut glacer nos bras avant qu'ils soient entrelacés.' "

The principles and practice of a life-time, however, are not so easily forgotten. Gray had never been one to abandon himself to grief: and, when the first shock occasioned by Bonstetten's departure was over, he did not do so now. Once again, as after West's death, good sense and self-discipline began to re-assert their influence. After all nothing had happened, so far as he could see, to shake his conviction that it was weak to waste one's time in unavailing lament, foolish not to try and distract oneself by occupation and rational pleasure, and shocking bad manners to worry one's friends by tedious complaining about one's own sorrows. How far he also called on his religion to strengthen his resolution we do not know. But it is interesting to find him, during the following months, attacking atheism with especial vehemence. Was not Hume's philosophy merely an excuse for yielding to one's desires, however reprehensible? As for the new French school of thinking—well, he was not feeling sufficiently well-disposed towards the French to regard them with any unnecessary charity! "Atheism is a vile dish," he said to Walpole, "though all the cooks of France combine to make new sauces to it. As to the soul, perhaps they may have none on the Continent; but I do think we have such things in England. Shakespeare, for example, I believe, had several to his share. As to the Jews—though they do not eat pork— I like them, because they are better Christians than Voltaire."

Determination was reinforced by habit. Gray's order of
living was, by now, second nature to him: and it was difficult
for him to break it. Even during the wretched days after
Bonstetten left, he contrived to make himself answer his
letters by return of post and keep his calendar of the seasons
up to date. After he got back from Suffolk, he took up his
old routine to all appearance as if nothing had happened:
read, made notes, took his daily walk to the Botanical
Gardens, dosed himself with sage tea, made arrangements
for his summer holiday—it was to be to the West Country
this time—composed letters to his friends in which, as before,
disquisitions on subjects of literary and historical interest are
relieved by delicately-drawn glimpses of landscape and
flashes of urbane humour. Now he is advising Mr. Beattie
the poet, on the principles of prosody, now giving Mr.
Warton of Oxford, the benefit of his researches into the early
English authors, now regaling Mason with tit-bits of Cambridge gossip—"Our friend Foljambe has resided in College
and persevered in the ways of godliness till about ten days ago,
when he disappeared; and no-one knows whether he is gone
a-hunting or a-fornicating"—now welcoming Nicholls and
his wife, with a graceful playfulness, to Cambridge: "Venga,
venga, si serva! I shall be proud to see you both. The lodgings
over the way will be empty, but such an entry, such a staircase! How will Mrs. N. be able to crowd through it? With
what grace, when she gets out of her chair, can she conduct
her hoop-petticoat through this auger-hole and up the dark
windings of the *grand escalier* that leads to her chamber?"
Even though his creative impulse might be dead, Gray the
artist in living, still managed to put up as technically finished a
performance as ever.

The fact that he did so reacted back on him. By behaving
as he had always behaved, Gray began to feel a little more as
he had been used to feel. If not happier, he grew calmer. And

all the more because the Bonstetten episode had been so brief: though the emotions it had roused in him had been uniquely violent, they simply had not had the time to cut so deep into him as those inspired by West and Walpole. After the first few weeks he did not go on missing Bonstetten as he had done, because he had not known him long enough to have acquired the habit of depending on his society. Moreover as the months passed and his usual mental atmosphere re-established itself, Gray's attitude to Bonstetten underwent a slight and subtle change: and all the more swiftly because Bonstetten had been irritatingly casual about answering his letters. He began to speak of him more in the tone in which he spoke of his other friends. This meant that he criticized him. There was no use, for instance, his blinking the fact that Bonstetten had a streak of silliness in him. He sent Gray his portrait—"You will think it was intended for his father," Gray told Nicholls; "doubtless he meant to look like an Englishman or an owl." Nor, now he was no longer under the spell of Bonstetten's actual presence, could Gray enter with full sympathy into the bewildering and melodramatic extravagance of Bonstetten's ever-changing moods. When some months later, Bonstetten, plunged on a sudden once more into temporary despair by the unconquerable philistin-ism of Berne society, wrote talking darkly of "un pistolet et du courage," Gray was more amused than concerned. "He is either disordered in his intellect—which is too possible," so he said—"or has done some strange thing that has exasper-ated his family and friends at home, which I am afraid is at least equally possible." Not that Gray had turned against Bonstetten. He still thought of him with tenderness and yearned to see him: and it is with an indulgent smile that he refers to his weaknesses. But no longer was he obsessed by him. Bonstetten had receded to a position in Gray's thoughts, from which his character could be surveyed with detachment.

Altogether by the autumn of 1770, to outward appearance, Gray was his old self again.

To outward appearance only, however. He was not really the same man as he had been a year before What he had been through had confirmed and intensified his melancholy. He had received another and painful proof of the precariousness of human joys: he had learnt that no amount of self-protective care can succeed in saving man from pain. The realization of this, coming at a time when he was no longer young, cast a new shadow over his brightest moments. Further, the whole experience had been a shock to his already shaken nervous system, from which he no longer had the strength completely to recover. He became more than ever a prey to hypochondria and nervous fears. In particular his sense of guilt at what he conceived to be his failure to carry out the obligations of his professorship, began to worry him more and more. By now he recognized that he would never be able to get his lecture finished: it would involve too great a strain. But then what should he do? It was sad to give up £400 a year: but it was more tolerable than to suffer perpetually from the pangs of conscience. He told Mason that he intended to resign.

Bonstetten was not solely responsible for his depression. There was also a physical cause for it. In the summer of 1770, the malady to which he had long been intermittently subject— it seems to have been some kind of kidney disease—took a serious turn for the worse. His recurrent fits of headache and dizziness became sharper and more frequent, and left him far more exhausted; with the result that he was permanently in a state of languor and lassitude. For the first time he suffered from what he called "mechanical low spirits", that is, low spirits induced purely by physical causes. Even an improvement in the weather did not make him feel better: this was a new thing in his life. The winter was one long gloom. When the spring did at last come, he felt as bad as ever. Surely, he began to wonder, this must mean that there was something dangerously wrong with him. A chilling premonition of death began to steal into his heart. He spoke of it to no-one. But it added a new and ominous darkness to the cloud that hung over him.

In March 1771 it was momentarily lightened by a flicker of brighter things. He got a letter from Nicholls saying that Bonstetten had written, inviting the two of them to spend part of the summer in Switzerland. Partly because he thought it might cheer Gray up, partly because he himself was delighted at the idea of breaking the monotony of a country clergyman's life by a continental holiday, Nicholls was enraptured with the proposal. "Let us go, my dear Gray, and leave low-thoughted care at the foot of the mountains; for the air above is too pure for it," he exclaimed in an access of refined enthusiasm. Gray was not unresponsive to his appeal. Though by now his feelings for Bonstetten were under control, he was not so detached as to have lost his longing to see him again. To revive the joys of the previous year, and amid that sublime Alpine scenery, through which in the flood of youthful hope he had passed with Walpole so long ago—wistfully he let his fancy play with so enchanting a prospect. For three months he hesitated: then in June, shortly before they were to start, he wrote to Nicholls to say that he had decided, after all, not to go. He felt too ill: and, he added, too sad. With his illness his depression had grown so settled that he no longer hoped it could be removed, even by seeing Bonstetten. More easily, perhaps, could he picture the pain he would feel, when for a second time, he would be forced to part from him. And had he not always made it his principle to avoid unnecessary pain? Better to stay quietly at Cambridge. Yet once again Gray's fear of misfortune had proved stronger than his expectation of happiness.

Nicholls came to see him before he set off. Gray made

him a characteristic request. Would he promise solemnly not to call on Voltaire while in Switzerland? "What could a visit from me signify?" asked Nicholls. "Every tribute to such a man signifies," replied Gray vehemently. Nicholls made, and conscientiously kept, the promise. Otherwise, excited no doubt by those care-dispelling properties in the mountain air on which he had expatiated to Gray, he seems to have let himself go, once he got abroad. He cast off clerical costume in favour of a waistcoat of flame-coloured satin with huge pockets, from which protruded a thermometer and a pair of spectacles. Thus attired, and to the astonishment of the sober Swiss, he paraded the shores of the Lake of Leman, meditating, in sentimental mood, on its association with La Nouvelle Heloise.

Gray would have enjoyed hearing about this: he always enjoyed hearing about the absurdities of his friends. But before any account could reach him, he was beyond earshot of human folly. On 24th July, while dining in College, he was seized with a fit of nausea that forced him to leave the Hall. Next day he was dangerously ill. Doctors were summoned: his friend Brown, now Master of Pembroke, and a young cousin of Gray's, Mary Antrobus, who was living at Cambridge, hastened to his bedside. But within a few days, it became clear to them that nothing could be done. It became clear to Gray too. For some time he had suspected that his end was near: and he had never been one to refuse to face painful facts. Not that it was a particularly painful fact to him. He had lost such will to live as he had ever possessed. All that remained was to try and quit the world with the same regard for order and comeliness as he had sought to live in it. He succeeded. Gray's last days were marked by an extraordinary composure. All sign of his fussiness and nervousness disappeared: only his clear sense and self-command remained. Though racked by violent convulsive fits, he managed, in a quiet interval, to give Brown precise instructions as to where to find his will, should it be needed: and one day, turning to his cousin who was sitting by his bed, "Molly, I shall die," he said calmly. On 30th July he breathed his last.

Mason came down from his home in York, to help Brown in settling Gray's affairs. It turned out to be an easy task. Gray's will and the instructions he had left for his funeral were as rationally devised and meticulously worded as his literary compositions has always been. In the middle of August when all was over Brown took a last look round Gray's rooms. Already every trace of his personality was gone from them. Mason had departed to York with the papers: furniture and pianoforte and blue vases had been packed and sent off to the various persons, to whom they were bequeathed. It looked, thought Brown sadly, like a place where no-one had lived for a very long time.

EPILOGUE

*I*T was late on an August afternoon, with the ebbing sunlight still a-glint on the white and gold of the book-cases and the tortoise-shell butterflies still flickering over the aster beds outside the window, that I finished this book. I sat back feeling contented: it is always agreeable to stop working. But I also felt sad. For I had grown to admire the two persons I had been writing about so much and to find the contemplation of their life so delightful that I hated saying good-bye to them. That I should feel like this was strange enough to start me reflecting. Melancholy, monotonous, thwarted, neither life was a delightful spectacle, as the phrase is generally understood. Nor were they themselves free from faults. Even the exquisite Dorothy could be both morbid and unreasonable: while as for Gray, what with his primness, his touchiness and his ludicrous nervous fads, he was in some respects downright tiresome. Moreover both were noticeably deficient in those social virtues by which the world professes to set such store. They found few human beings likeable: corporate activities were all they most abhorred. However none of this made me like or admire them less. Could it be that steady nerves and social usefulness were not in fact the qualities in other people that most make us feel ourselves inferior to them? Was it not rather some unusual fineness of nature; an eye for the truth, depth and delicacy of feeling, the presence to be detected in them of a strong and beautiful inner life? These Dorothy and Gray possessed. It was because their hearts were so civilized that they found the world so barbarous: their melancholy arose in part from the fact that they never committed the blasphemy of thinking human existence adequate to satisfy the aspirations of the soul. Whatever their defects, they were never hard or shallow or godless. Or dull: the clear twilight, in which they lived, gleamed and trembled with the play of their

193

humour and their imagination: those two qualities, which more than all others, distinguish the man from the animal. And with what enchanting an eloquence did they present them to the world! Their every utterance is as deft and graceful as the flicker of the butterflies over the aster beds.

After all, I thought, it was no wonder that I sought their company so ardently: and, as the sunlight ebbed ever more palely over the book-cases, that I said good-bye to them with regret.